MALCOLM ARNOLD
An Introduction to his Music

MALCOLM ARNOLD
An Introduction to his Music

HUGO COLE

FABER MUSIC
IN ASSOCIATION WITH
FABER AND FABER
LONDON AND BOSTON

© 1989 by Hugo Cole
First published in 1989 by Faber Music Ltd
in association with Faber & Faber Ltd
3 Queen Square London WC1N 3AU
Typesetting by Pageproof Ltd, Newmarket
Music drawn by Sheila Stanton
Cover design by M & S Tucker
Printed and bound in Great Britain by
Mackays of Chatham PLC, Chatham, Kent

CONTENTS

v

ACKNOWLEDGEMENTS

For permission to reproduce extracts from works by Malcolm Arnold, grateful thanks
are due to the following copyright owners:

Campbell Connelly & Co. Ltd - *The Key* (Copyright © 1958 by Columbia Pictures
Music Corp, USA. Words by Al Stillman)

The Composer - *Electra* Op. 79, *Fantasy for Audience and Orchestra* Op. 106, *The Open
Window* Op. 56, *Women in our Time*

EMI Music Publishing Ltd and International Music Publications - *Five William Blake
Songs* Op. 66 (© 1966 by EMI Music Publishing Ltd), *The Reckoning* (© 1969 by Screen
Gems - EMI Music Ltd), *Song of Freedom* Op. 109 © 1974 by B. Feldman and Co. Ltd)

Faber Music Ltd - *Concerto No. 2 for Clarinet and Orchestra* Op. 115, *Concerto No. 2 for
Flute and Orchestra* Op. 111, *Concerto for Trumpet and Orchestra* Op. 125, *Concerto for Two
Pianos (Three Hands) and Orchestra* Op. 104, *Concerto for Two Violins and String Orchestra*
Op. 77, *Concerto for Viola and Chamber Orchestra* Op. 108, *Concerto for 28 Players* Op. 105,
Duo for Flute and Viola Op. 10, *The Fair Field* Op. 110, *Fantasy on a Theme of John Field* Op.
116, *Larch Trees* Op. 3, *Oboe Quartet* Op. 61, *Peterloo* Op. 97, *Philharmonic Concerto* Op.
120, *Rinaldo and Armida* Op. 49, *Sonata for Flute and Piano* Op. 121, *Song of Simeon* Op.
69, *String Quartet No. 2* Op. 118, *Symphonic Study: Machines* Op. 30, *Symphony No. 6* Op.
95, *Symphony No. 7* Op. 113, *Symphony No. 8* Op. 124, *Symphony for Brass Instruments*
Op. 123, *Variations for Orchestra on a Theme of Ruth Gipps* Op. 122

Alfred Lengnick & Co. Ltd - *Beckus the Dandipratt* Op. 5, *Concerto for Clarinet and
Strings* Op. 20, *English Dances (Set 2)* Op. 33, *Serenade for Small Orchestra* Op. 26, *Sonata
No. 1 for Violin and Piano* Op. 15, *Sonata for Viola and Piano* Op. 17, *Sonatina for Clarinet
and Piano* Op. 29, *Sonatina for Flute and Piano* Op. 19, *Sonatina for Oboe and Piano* Op. 28,
String Quartet No. 1 Op. 23, *Symphony No. 1* Op. 22

Paterson's Publications Ltd and Peters Edition Ltd - *Concerto for Flute and Strings*
Op. 45, *Concerto for Guitar and Chamber Orchestra* Op. 67, *Concerto for Harmonica and
Orchestra* Op. 46, *Concerto for Piano Duet and Strings* Op. 32, *Five Pieces for Violin and
Piano* Op. 84, *Four Scottish Dances* Op. 59, *A Grand, Grand Overture* Op. 57, *Homage to the
Queen* Op. 42, *John Clare Cantata* Op. 52, *Piano Trio* Op. 54, *Quintet for Brass* Op. 73,
Quintet for Flute, Violin, Viola, Horn and Bassoon Op. 7, *Sinfonietta No. 2* Op. 65,
Sinfonietta No. 3 Op. 81, *Sonata No. 2 for Violin and Piano* Op. 43, *Symphony No. 2* Op. 40,
Symphony No. 3 Op. 63, *Symphony No. 4* Op. 71, *Symphony No. 5* Op. 74, *Three Shanties
for Wind Quintet* Op. 4, *Toy Symphony* Op. 62

Roberton Publications - *Piano Sonata in B minor*

Grateful thanks are also due to Faber Music Ltd for permission to reproduce an extract
from 'The Fly' from *Songs and Proverbs of William Blake* Op. 74 by Benjamin Britten

FOREWORD

Malcolm Arnold has often been the victim, not so much of misrepresentation as of partial representation. He has been judged and categorised (as were Poulenc and Prokofiev before him) almost entirely on the strength of a few, much-played, popular works. There has been next to no informed discussion of many of his more substantial works, of the varied and often highly original compositional processes employed, or of the ways in which his musical character has developed over the years.

As a result, we share no broadly-based perspective or common ground of understanding, as we do in the case of those of his contemporaries, traditionalists or avant-gardists, whose works – judged 'significant' for whatever reason – are regularly analysed and assessed from many different viewpoints. This puts a greater load of responsibility on the writer whose opinions can't be set off against those of others. But that is no reason for suppressing personal opinions, or for acting as council for the defence – all too many articles and books about composers lose credibility when the author over-zealously 'makes a case' for x or y. I have allowed myself to express enthusiasm for the works I most admire and have not stifled reservations about those which I admire less. But I would stress that even 'description' and 'analysis' can be undertaken from many points of view, and that 'evaluation' in particular can never be objective. Someone has to write the First Words about Arnold's lesser-known works; the Last Word, happily for us all, will never be written.

This first detailed survey of the music covers concert works, opera, ballet, the more substantial of the many special-occasion pieces, and a sample selection of the film scores. Incidental music for theatre, television and radio, shorter occasional pieces and fanfares have been passed over. I hope that the book may be useful to performers wanting to enrich their repertories and may stimulate others to make closer acquaintance with the Unknown Arnold. More generally, my aim has been to portray Arnold's character as a composer, and to chart the course of its development, through discussion of the music.

The works-index includes only works mentioned in the text, with a note of the publishers. A comprehensive works list with details of instrumentation, first performances, discography and bibliography may be found in Alan Poulton's catalogue, *The Music of Malcolm Arnold* (Faber Music). Standard pitch symbols, as defined in the Oxford and Harvard Dictionaries of Music, are used.

All thanks to the staffs of the British Music Information Centre, the Royal College of Music Library, the National Sound Archive, the National Film Institute and the London Library for unfailing courtesy and help. To Arnold's several publishers, who have made material freely available to me; to Georgina Ivor, who has been tireless in supplying me with scores, tapes and information; to Alan Poulton, whose catalogue has saved me many hours of labour. To Sally Cavender and Patrick Carnegy of Faber Music, who were between them responsible for commissioning the book, also to Wendy Thompson and Tim Roberts, who saw it through the press. Lastly to Malcolm Arnold himself, for the geniality and patience with which he has answered many questions, and for the music which is the subject of this book.

1

MAINLY BIOGRAPHICAL

Malcolm Arnold was born in Northampton on 21 October 1921. His father was a prosperous shoe manufacturer, also an amateur pianist and organist with a great love of music. His mother, a good musician and an excellent pianist and accompanist, was also the great-granddaughter of William Hawes (1785-1846); Master of the Chapel Royal, composer of glees and madrigals, the conductor who had introduced Weber's *Der Freischütz* to English audiences, himself adding extra arias.

Some of Arnold's earliest memories are of his mother's singing and playing. The youngest child of four, he was brought up in a strictly religious home in which children who didn't go to church on Sundays were caned. The family intention had been that he should go to Mill Hill, the public school to which many well-off Nonconformists sent their children at that time (Mr Arnold was a Primitive Methodist). Arnold resisted the idea strongly. He already hated school discipline, which, he said, 'put ideas of study out of my mind'. In the end he was allowed to stay at home, to be tutored by one of his aunts. She too was an excellent musician and a good viola player (in earlier years she had also taught him the violin). He first learned piano with another aunt; then went to study with Philip Pfaff, organist of St Matthew's, Northampton, who gave him a solid grounding in modal counterpoint and encouraged him to compose. Pfaff earned Arnold's lasting gratitude for his wise and conscientious teaching.

When he was twelve, enthusiasm for jazz, and in particular for the playing of Louis Armstrong, led him to take up the trumpet. By the time he was fifteen he was travelling to London for private lessons with Ernest Hall, paid for by the exhibition fund of the Guildhall School of Music. Two years later, he won a scholarship to the Royal College of Music, where he again studied trumpet with Hall. He was to have gone to Patrick Hadley for composition, but Hadley was then in poor health, and he went instead to Gordon Jacob.

Jacob was a kindly and knowledgeable teacher, from whom he learned much, particularly in matters of instrumentation and the voicing of parts. But Ernest Hall was the man who taught him most, and whom he most admired for wisdom and musicianship. He also studied piano with J. Hurst Bannister. Arnold never aspired to be a serious pianist, but could amuse people at parties and has always enjoyed playing jazz.

Before the end of his second year at the RCM, having won second prize in the Cobbett Competition with a one-movement quartet, he left to join the London Philharmonic Orchestra as second trumpet, and began the third, and perhaps most important phase of his education as a composer. During his orchestral years, Arnold came to know the symphonic repertory from the inside, playing under many of the world's greatest conductors. He now made first acquaintance with many of the works that were most to influence him, not from the scores, but from the live sounds. It was after the LPO had played a movement of Mahler's Second Symphony that he rushed off to Foyle's Bookshop to buy all the Mahler scores he could lay hands on. During the long *tacets* which fall to the lot of all brass players, he had leisure to listen, and to discover at first hand what worked and what didn't work in matters of instrumentation. He learned too from the friends in the orchestra who tried out his first chamber works, written to stave off boredom on long wartime tours. The first work in which Arnold now recognizes his true composing self was *Larch Trees*, completed in June 1943, a year after he had joined the LPO.

At the start of the war, Arnold had been a conscientious objector. He was directed into the Fire Service, but when the offer to join the LPO came along, he was exempted from other war duty. By 1943 he had succeeded John Cozens as principal trumpet, but was growing increasingly restless. In the same year he left the orchestra to volunteer, first for the navy, which could find no place for him, then for the army, ending up in the regiment of the Buffs.

Arnold himself had said that he left the LPO in reaction against orchestral discipline – another manifestation, maybe, of the instinct that had led him to reject the idea of public school and later, when at the RCM, to run away to Plymouth with the idea that he would lead the life of an artisan. There he was discovered by private detectives playing in a dance band and was returned to the College, where the tolerant Principal, Sir George Dyson, welcomed him back. The army career ended even more dramatically when Arnold was directed into the Buffs band and decided, in protest, to shoot himself in the foot. The sergeant who had been making his life a burden fainted when he discovered him in the lavatory, in a pool of his own blood.

After four weeks in hospital Arnold was discharged from the army and returned to trumpet playing. For a short time, he played second to Ernest Hall in the BBC Symphony Orchestra, then rejoined the LPO, remaining principal trumpet until 1948, when he won the Mendelssohn Scholarship and abandoned professional playing for good.

Between 1943 and 1948, Arnold had composed almost twenty concert works, including the comedy overture *Beckus the Dandipratt*, the first clarinet concerto (Concerto for Clarinet and Strings), and several chamber works which still rank among his best. Eduard van Beinum recorded *Beckus* with the LPO in 1948, while Arnold was still with the orchestra. By now, Lengnick was publishing his music, and he was beginning to write for film, having already in 1947 provided music for several documentaries (his first feature, *Badger's Green*, followed in 1948). He had also married Sheila Nicholson, a violinist who had trained at the Royal Academy of Music, and in 1948 their daughter Katherine was born. By the time he won the Mendelssohn Scholarship, Arnold had already acquired something of a reputation as a composer as well as considerable family responsibilities.

On Dyson's advice, Arnold headed for Italy, but with no intention of submitting himself to further instruction. The few months spent there during 1948 did not affect his outlook or musical character in any appreciable way. But he loved the country and heard plenty of music, forming a poor opinion of Italian concert life but acquiring a taste for pasta and frascati before returning to England to start life as a full-time professional composer. This was a daunting enough prospect in a country where the number of 'serious' composers earning a living from music could at that time have been counted on the fingers of one hand. But Arnold had confidence, versatility, and practical know-how as well as native talent, and never had cause to regret the leap he had taken.

From 1948 until the early 1960s Arnold's productivity was at its peak. The First Symphony was completed in 1949, the Second in 1952: a marvellous year for Arnold, in which he came to be recognized as one of the brightest hopes of English music. The Second Symphony, first performed at Bournemouth in May under the direction of Arnold's staunch supporter Charles Groves, was enthusiastically received by public and critics, and was soon off on its travels round the world. In June, Arnold's first ballet, the full-length *Homage to the Queen*, received its first performance at Covent Garden on Queen Elizabeth II's coronation day and was also well received. The two sets of *English Dances* (the second set had been published in 1951) were by this time proving to be immensely popular with amateur and professional orchestras.

The commissions now poured in at an ever-increasing rate; in the mid-fifties, Arnold was often bracketed with Benjamin Britten and William Walton as one of the three highest-earning 'serious' composers in the country. Third, Fourth and Fifth Symphonies (all commissioned) followed in 1957, 1960 and 1961. There was a steady output of slighter orchestral works: overtures, dance sets and divertimentos, and a few more chamber works; while Arnold was always ready to write concertos, sonatas and sonatinas for players he particularly admired. Between 1952 and 1960 Arnold wrote three more ballets (all for Covent Garden) and a one-act opera. As if that wasn't enough, he was for most of this period one of the busiest film composers in the country, turning out the scores for upwards of six feature films a year at a rate that terrified others working in the same field.

At the same time, he appeared with increasing frequency as conductor of his own works in the concert hall and in film and recording studios. Renewed contact with the orchestra gave him much delight, and he knew well how to get the best out of his players without waste of time or words. He was soon being invited to conduct programmes which included works other than his own.

Philip Jones, at one time principal trumpet of the New Philharmonia, remembers a performance of Berlioz's *Symphonie Fantastique* that Arnold conducted at Croydon as the finest and most exciting in which he ever played. Arnold was still never too busy to find time for the composition of orchestral joke pieces on the grand scale for the Hoffnung concerts, or the many flourishes and fanfares for special occasions that appear in the opus list alongside the serious works.

Well before 1960, however, critics were beginning to ask whether Arnold was a 'serious' composer at all. His willingness to cross stylistic frontiers, not only to flirt with the idioms of commercial music but to embrace them wholeheartedly, and his often belligerent rejection of 'experimental' music in all its manifestations, led to the steady undermining of his reputation in musical-intellectual circles. This was a time when younger critics were reacting against the traditionalist attitudes and insularity of their elders, when 'diatonic' had become as dirty a word as 'romantic' had been in the 1920s and 1930s, when young composers who did not adopt serial methods were liable to be written off as of little account. Meanwhile, the extraordinary popularity of such works as the Three Shanties for Wind Quintet, the *English Dances* and the comedy overtures, together with the comparative neglect of the symphonies and chamber works, led even his admirers to regard him as the jester of English music, or as a sort of *idiot savant* who in his innocence sometimes achieved feats beyond the powers of more sophisticated and worldly-wise composers.

Arnold served a year and a half as Chairman of the Composers' Guild, during which time he devoted much time and energy to the question of composers' film contracts – because of the anxiety of many composers to get film work at all costs, the results of his work were meagre. At the same time, he remained a fairly lonely figure among composers and a member of no group or clique. He had never been one of the gang of learned clerks who read *Perspectives of New Music* and thought in terms of magic squares or compositional matrices. So far from issuing manifestos to explain or justify his music, he preferred, in interviews or programme notes, to cover his tracks and to discuss almost anything rather than the structural processes involved.

This may partly explain why his ingenious uses and adaptations of serial procedures so often escaped the notice of critics; though it is equally probable that those who had already attached a 'traditionalist' label to Arnold's music were psychologically incapable of perceiving it in any other light. He was given little credit for his experiments in varying the symphonic mix, while the introduction of popular elements into 'serious' works tended to alienate the traditionalists who had once been his supporters as well as the radicals. But he remained on good terms with the BBC's Controller of Music, William Glock, who commissioned both the Fourth Symphony and the Fantasy for Audience and Orchestra, performed on the Last Night of the Proms in 1970. (Later, under Robert Ponsonby's regime, Arnold fell into disfavour; there were no more BBC commissions and Proms performances of any but his lightest works ceased altogether.)

By the sixties, there were also personal problems to be faced. The pace at which Arnold had been living and working could not be kept up for ever. There were periods of depression, from which he took refuge in heavy drinking, and his marriage broke up. Though he continued intermittently to produce works of quality and to compose three or four feature films most years until 1966, 1962–66 were lean years from the compositional point of view. He left his Richmond home and moved, first to Thursley, a village near Haslemere, then, in the mid-sixties, to Cornwall, where he settled with his second wife Isabel at St Merryn.

Arnold loved Cornwall and the Cornish and became closely involved in local musical activities. His *Padstow Lifeboat* march became a sort of signature tune for several Cornish bands; in 1968 he organized at Truro Cathedral a festival of the music of Thomas Merritt, the Cornish copper miner and organist (1863-1908), newly scored for large forces including two brass bands. In 1968 he was made a Bard of the Cornish Gorseth, an honour of which he is particularly proud. (Two years later he was awarded the CBE; he also holds honorary doctorates of music from Exeter, Durham, and Leicester Universities.)

Arnold's rate of composition was never again to approach that of the fifties; but the flow of substantial works continued. The Sixth Symphony, the Viola Concerto, the Concerto for Two Pianos (Three Hands), the Concerto for 28 Players and the *Song of Freedom* all belong to the Cornish years.

Arnold had lost none of his exuberance or gusto for life at this period; but memories of the critics' harsh attacks rankled. When, in 1971, Christopher Ford went to St Merryn to interview Arnold for the *Guardian*, he was greeted with boisterous *bonhomie*, nobly entertained, taken the round of local pubs, while his host discoursed on every subject under the sun. But when Ford asked if Arnold felt any bitterness against the critics, the answer was: 'I'll tell you how bitter I am – only as bitter as a man who wants to stand up and walk down the street and doesn't want people shouting offensive, patronizing remarks after him. The critics have got to live, but for Christ's sake why don't they let me live too?'

In 1972 Arnold uprooted himself once more and moved with his family to Dublin, where he remained until 1977. The Seventh Symphony, the *Fantasy on a Theme of John Field*, the Second Clarinet Concerto and the Second String Quartet were all written or completed in Ireland. Arnold's pleasure in identifying with his place of residence is reflected in his use of one of the loveliest of Field's nocturnes in the *Fantasy*, and in the introduction of an Irish jig in the Second Quartet – a compliment to his adopted country and to Hugh Maguire, leader of the Allegri String Quartet and a noted folk fiddler. Echoes of Irish music can be heard too in the last movement of the Seventh Symphony and in the first movement of the Eighth.

In 1977, Arnold returned to England. His second marriage had ended disastrously, he himself was 'flat on his back', and for long periods during the next few years was hospitalized or incapable of work. The only pieces completed between 1978 and 1986 were the Symphony for Brass Instruments, the Eighth Symphony and the Trumpet Concerto.

In the mid-eighties, he has emerged into calmer waters. He has settled at Wymondham near Norwich and has again begun to compose and conduct. He has completed a set of *Irish Dances* that had been long on the stocks, has written his Ninth Symphony, a fantasy and concerto for the Danish recorder player Michala Petri and a cello work for Julian Lloyd Webber. He is also, much to his own satisfaction, increasingly involved in local musical activities. As he said to Stewart Orr in a sixty-fifth birthday interview: 'You've got to be local somewhere . . . you should learn the traditions of a place. I wish I'd found Norfolk sooner!'

2

APPRENTICE YEARS

On the manuscript cover of the song-cycle *Kensington Gardens* (completed in 1938, and the first extended work to survive) an older and more critical Arnold has written: 'Words by Humbert Wolfe; Music(?) by Malcolm Arnold'. It is true enough that these nine songs have no very striking message to convey, and that they are clearly the works of a composer of limited resources. Yet already there are hints of what is to come, intimations of Arnold's later character appearing as much in what is not done as in what is done.

Textures are spare, vocal or piano part often being reduced to a single unsupported melodic line. There are conventional arpeggio accompaniment figures, but none of those aimless filling-in parts with which unconfident composers are apt to overload their scores. Words are set with almost exaggerated respect for verbal rhythms and inflexions, while the piano mostly keeps to its own independent figurations. The mild and fanciful spirit of the poems is faithfully reflected in a few of the more whimsical songs. A crusty old gardener is characterized in a few bars of limping 5/8, a mock-serious dialogue between a chestnut and a beech tree set against a solemn piano chorale. The forms are clear, even when the composer has not yet discovered the way to fill them out with real music.

There is nothing impracticable in the handful of early piano pieces; also nothing to suggest that Arnold's imagination or powers of invention were particularly stimulated by the instrument. Two Ernest Dowson settings for five-part choir *a cappella* show sophisticated use of close chromatic harmony – a first and last trace of Delius's influence in Arnold's music. These early manuscripts are clearly and firmly written, well laid out and sensibly phrased; by no means the work of a beginner. The aspiring composer was already a practical musician, who found no difficulty in transcribing sounds into symbols.

The Phantasy for String Quartet of 1941 shows Arnold well on the way to professionalism, handling the medium confidently and resourcefully, by no means overawed by the thought that he was following in the footsteps of the great masters of chamber music. Who but Arnold would have entered for the annual Cobbett Prize Competition a quartet opening with a tango? The main theme is catchy and well devised for strings, with suspense built into certain long-sustained notes. A second theme is too obviously designed to go into counterpoint with the first, while the solemn subject of the central *Andante* is hardly characterful enough to stand up to the full treatment it receives, building up twice to grandiose *fortissimo* climaxes. The last section is much more interesting: a one-in-a-bar scherzo with Beethoven-like syncopations, cross-rhythms, and obsessive repetitions of short motives. The section is conceived in true quartet style, the roles of instruments constantly changing, new alliances set and dissolved from moment to moment, impetus maintained through just on 300 bars of 3/4 *presto*. Arnold pays homage to Beethoven less happily in the final pages, where reminiscences of earlier sections precede the final *Molto presto*, itself quite ingeniously based on the tango theme. It is the first, but not the last, of Arnold's works to show signs of haste in the making (it was in fact written between 6 June and 17 June, no doubt to meet the competition deadline). Arnold himself seems to have regarded the quartet as expendable, since in the same year he anatomized it, incorporating the final section into the Wind Quintet Op. 2 (now lost).

The Piano Sonata of 1942, economical and precise in musical draughtsmanship, keeps up an easy, conversational flow through its three concise movements. Even if he has at the moment nothing very urgent to say, Arnold is in command of his resources, calling the tune rather than drifting on the current of reminiscent inspiration in the manner of many embryo composers. The first movement opens with a melodic ostinato which supports a longer *cantabile,* one thing leading to another in a very natural and spontaneous manner until the arrival of a second, contrasted, theme.

Ex.1

In the development Arnold makes use of a compositional procedure often found in Haydn and Mozart, in which some cliché accompaniment figure (in this case recurring tonic–dominant quavers) is upgraded to become a motive in its own right. A short, severely plain, and somewhat faceless slow movement leads to a lively and grotesque *Alla marcia.* As in the first movement, there are extended passages in bare two-part counterpoint; but the higher dissonance level and the character of the harmonically unstable main theme seem to indicate the influence of Prokofiev or early Hindemith:

Ex.2

The way in which interest is rekindled at a late stage with a new dotted-rhythm theme is very much in character. Like Haydn, Arnold is able to put himself in the listener's shoes, knowing well that constant stimulation, in the form of shocks, surprises, new ideas and new treatments, is needed if full involvement is to be assured. The style of piano writing, unidiomatic but not antipianistic, is also characteristic of Arnold. The notes lie nicely under the fingers; but the Sonata could as well (or even better) be a reduction of an instrumental work as piano music in its own right.

The Sonata for Flute and Piano of 1942 is the first of Arnold's hybrid works: a predominantly tonal piece which makes sporadic use of serial techniques. These are used in the first movement to generate one or two angular melodies and one ingenious accompaniment figure, while in the slow movement they give rise to a few decorative arabesques. The last movement is a cheerful *Allegro*, tonal but with some mischievous distortions of expectable harmonies. The mixing of idioms is not too convincing; we are aware of gear changes when the music moves into serial mode, while the main themes have a manufactured feel to them, something that is rare enough in works of any period. Arnold himself seems to have decided that the serial signpost was likely to lead him into a blind alley, and showed no inclination to explore that particular path further at this stage in his career.

Larch Trees Op. 3 was completed in June 1943, by which time Arnold had been with the LPO for almost a year. It was first heard at the Royal Albert Hall in October 1943 at a rehearsal of new works organized by the Committee for the Promotion of New Music (later the SPNM), Arnold himself conducting the LPO. Scoring is for normal woodwind, four horns and strings; there are no changes of metre or tempo (4/4; *Andante con moto*) throughout its nine-minute length.

The mood of this miniature tone poem is set in the introductory
nine bars, in which flutes and bassoons softly reiterate a Debussyan
chromatic figure against the sustained octaves of muted horns, **Ex. 3a**.
Violins twice hint at the main theme before launching into a long
stream of unbroken melody which is passed around the orchestra, **Ex.
3b**, building to a broad climax before the chromatic figures of the
introduction return in a peaceful epilogue:

Ex.3a

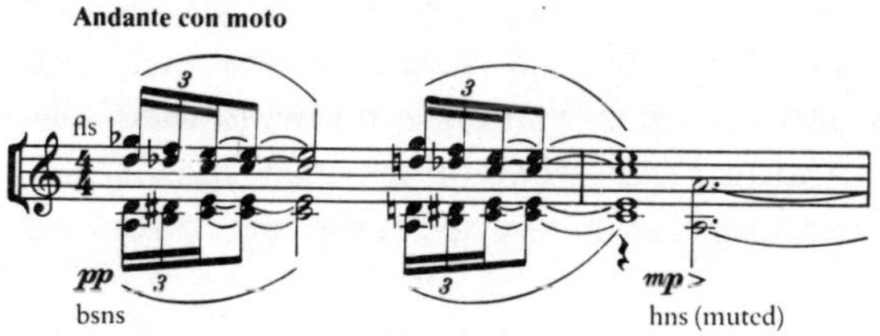

Ex.3b

It is at once apparent that Arnold has discovered a medium in
which he can work with total assurance, and that stimulates and abets
his creative powers. The characters of the instruments are knowingly
exploited, as are their differing natures in various ranges and at
various dynamic levels. The expressive possibilities of many types of
articulation are recognized in music that is notated with Mahlerian
precision. The third-based harmony is relatively simple; but Arnold
establishes the relative values on his consonance–dissonance scale
with full assurance. Some passages may look startlingly bare of action

to the motive hunter. But Arnold knows well where the music needs to pause for breath, for how long a single held note can command attention, and how a change of timbre can refresh the listener as effectively as a change of harmony or metre.

Arnold again makes use of the Haydnish procedure noted in the Piano Sonata. A falling octave at first appears to be no more than a cadential formula later claims attention as a motive in its own right, at the same time acting as an unobtrusive connecting link with what has gone before. Already, Arnold is a knowing craftsman rather than an innocent trusting to luck and instinct. His talent for devising long spans of easy-flowing melody is put to good use in a work that is, in effect, one long melody. And one distinctive 'fingerprint' can already be clearly identified; variants of motive x will crop up again and again in Arnold's music.

Yet if one were not already in the know, who would one guess the composer to be? Some disciple of Debussy? William Alwyn in one of his Frencher moods? It is quite hard to recognize the Arnold one knows in this mellifluous, dreamy, atmospheric piece. There is, however, one good reason why *Larch Trees* should appear to be a one-off work, in a category of its own. It was the only Arnold piece to have been inspired by contemplation of the natural world; the impulse to write it sprang direct from Arnold's delight in a glade of larch trees he discovered on a Yorkshire holiday.

In the next two works in the opus list we hear for the first time a tone of voice that is unmistakably Arnold's own. The Three Shanties for Wind Quintet Op. 4, also of 1943, are the first of a group of entertainment pieces, written for friends in the LPO to play on wartime tours (which explains why the first performance was given at Filton Aerodrome, near Bristol). The first and last of the three seem to have been modelled on Gordon Jacob's arrangements of well-known tunes made for Tommy Handley's wartime radio series ITMA ('It's That Man Again'). The tunes of 'What shall we do with the drunken sailor?' and 'Johnny come down to Hilo' are paraded in many guises, the former at one point converted into a tango, the latter to a rumba.

No one is likely to miss the perky syncopations and rhythmic distortions, fuguing treatments, the sailor's drunken hiccups, or the *Klangfarbenmelodie* transformation of 'Johnny', shared out note by note between the instruments:

Ex. 4

But Arnold avoids the more obvious bassoon jokes, and there is art as well as humour in the way he irons out the sailor's tune, **Ex. 5a**, into oscillating triplets while maintaining the thematic connection, **Ex. 5b**, reduces the theme to its bare essentials in an episode led by horn, **Ex. 5c**, or retains the rhythm as an anchor when the theme is momentarily left behind, **Ex. 5d**:

Ex. 5a

Ex. 5b

Ex. 5c

Ex. 5d

By such means, he creates a real little movement out of what might have been a series of musical jests at the sailor's expense. Arnold handles this awkward combination of instruments with tact and a precise sense of character, observing their limitations, taking advantage of their odder aptitudes and of the ways in which timbres blend or stand apart at different dynamic levels and in different registers.

The central movement is grave and simple, the scoring a model of restraint and economy; Arnold already knows which notes to leave out as well as which to put in. The tune 'Boney was a warrior' is repeated six times unvaried over the lightest of accompaniments, the tune given in turn to (muted) horn; flute; bassoon; flute; clarinet; horn again. The oboe has no more than a dozen harmony-filling notes.

Beckus the Dandipratt Op. 5, Arnold's first work for symphony orchestra, was completed in 1943, though not performed until two years later, when it was broadcast by the BBC Scottish Orchestra under Ian Whyte's direction. Arnold himself played in the first public performance, given by the LPO under Eduard van Beinum at the Royal Opera House, Covent Garden, on 16 November 1947, and also in the subsequent recording. *Beckus* could be described as a scherzo-overture; and is in fact the ancestor of several of Arnold's symphonic scherzos. But (as in Strauss's *Till Eulenspiegel*) the comedy is shot through with unease. The Dandipratt ('a small, insignificant or contemptible fellow': OED) has two main themes, stated early in the work. Note the dissonant background harmony that qualifies the cornet's apparently confident statement of the first:

Ex.6

(continued)

It is just as well that the main features of this theme are memorable in themselves, since it is booked to suffer many adventures and misadventures; sometimes assaulted violently from without, sometimes losing the thread of its own arguments or repeating endlessly a single bar. The cornet theme, like the main theme of Till, is fragmented, though transformations are less thoroughgoing and methodical. The Dandipratt never quite loses his identity; he does not triumph over adversity, but neither does he succumb; after each calamity he reappears, again like Till, unreformed and apparently unconcerned – saved perhaps by his own insignificance.

Till has already twice found his way into this account of Beckus, and there is an obvious if superficial resemblance between the opening gambits of both main themes. But Arnold stands closer to Berlioz than to Strauss in his compositional processes, in the clarity and transparency of his orchestration, almost without doublings, in the comparative absence of counterpoint, and in the character of his orchestral generalship – in the way, for instance, in which he will hold his heavy forces in reserve for long passages of chamber-music transparency, then suddenly throw in the whole of the brass section in some shock attack. The use of cornet, not a standard instrument in English orchestras, suggests French influence; *Le Carnaval Romain* was surely somewhere at the back of Arnold's mind while he was writing his own overture. Arnold himself mentions Sibelius as having provided the model for a long development passage in which fragments of themes are deployed against a long-sustained *pianissimo* drum roll. But Sibelius is about the last name one would think of in connection with *Beckus*. Already, Arnold has progressed to the point where influences are fully digested before they emerge in his own music.

Whatever the ingredients that went into the pot, the overture that resulted is quintessential Arnold: a work that only one man could possibly have written, which shows no signs of uncertainty or immaturity. *Beckus*, moreover, does not follow the pattern of British comedy overtures, in which the composer traditionally allows himself a breathing space in the form of a lyrical central episode (as in Elgar's *Cockaigne*, Ireland's *London Overture*, Bax's *Overture to a Picaresque Comedy*, Rawsthorne's *Street Corner*, Alwyn's *Derby Day*, and others too numerous to mention); impetus is maintained unchecked throughout its eight-and-a-half-minute length. To keep the music spinning along with so much verve for so long demands wit and imagination, technical resource, and a rare ability to exploit the possibilities of the developing musical situation.

Arnold, a comparatively late starter, was no youthful prodigy; it is easy to think of any number of composers who had written works as accomplished and as individual by the time they were twenty-two. But if we compare *Beckus* with the song-cycle, piano pieces, and quartet discussed earlier in this chapter, his achievement seems more remarkable. In five years, he had mastered the traditional arts of orchestration, had developed subtle and sophisticated skills in the structuring of music. He was ready to enter the lists as a fully professional composer; one who had already proved that he had something new and special to offer the world.

3

VOYAGES OF DISCOVERY
Concert Works 1943–52

The decade from 1944 to 1953 was a time of much activity for Arnold in
which he moved out into new areas, seizing every chance to extend
his expressive and technical range, and discovering in the process
special aptitudes which in earlier years had lain dormant. The
characters of works of this period can be linked quite closely to the
contexts of composition. Thus, the earlier chamber works, written for
the diversion of friends with little thought of public performance, are
a good deal less 'severe' (in the eighteenth-century sense) than those
produced after 1946, which tend to be more concise, more clearly
structured, making dramatic and rhetorical points more cogently. The
Violin and Viola Sonatas, the Symphony for Strings, the Clarinet
Concerto and the First Quartet are the works of a composer eager to
demonstrate his powers, not afraid to advance into new territory,
even at the risk of causing distress to conventional or timid listeners.

At the same time, these works of the late 1940s are often abstract in
more senses than one. In the most obvious sense, they are abstract
because they follow no extra-musical programmes; next, because
Arnold had not yet perfected the art of tailoring works to suit the
characters of particular performers. Lastly, they are abstract in that the
message seems to be directed to no particular group of listeners. In
the late forties few outlets were available to young and little-known
composers seeking public performance, and Arnold's early chamber
works were of necessity first performed at Committee for the
Promotion of New Music (CPNM) concerts or at small-scale chamber
concerts, with occasional broadcasts heard by the far-removed and

unknowable radio audience. In so far as Arnold was at this time writing for anyone at all, he was writing for the specialized contemporary-music élite, but even more, one suspects, for himself.

By the end of the 1940s, however, Arnold was writing for many of the most distinguished players in the country, and the chamber works were increasingly reflecting the characters of the performers for whom they were first destined. At the same time, the tone of voice becomes more genial. The Sonatinas and the Divertimento for flute, oboe and clarinet blend the 'galant' and 'learned' in delightful manner. Arnold seems to be developing a distinct idea of the sort of listener he would like to reach: not the earnest intellectual of the new-music concerts, but someone more in the mould of the prototypical Promenader.

It was only after he had left the London Philharmonic Orchestra in 1948 to become a full-time composer that commissions for works for full orchestra started to come Arnold's way. At this time too he became heavily involved in writing for films: producing eleven scores in 1948, fifteen in 1949 (including four feature films), and about eight a year for the following four years. Two orchestral scores of this period, (Symphonic Study: *Machines* Op. 30 and *The Sound Barrier* Op. 38) derive directly from film scores. The other shorter works: two overtures and the two sets of *English Dances* represent Arnold at his least problematical. He has learned how to write simply and directly in ways that the least sophisticated audiences can appreciate, without losing his own musical character in the process.

There are also a few piano pieces designed for children and some psalm settings from this period, as well as a one-act comic opera *The Dancing Master* Op. 34, which still awaits professional stage performance. All of these seem to lie well off the main line of Arnold's development, and will be considered later.

Early Chamber Works

The Quintet for Flute, Violin, Viola, Horn and Bassoon Op. 7 and the Duo for Flute and Viola Op.10 are easy-going, informal works, avoiding big 'public' gestures, demanding no great virtuosity from the players, resembling Haydn's more intimate quartets in their conversational character and the unpredictable freedom of thematic developments. Interest lies in the dialogue itself rather than in any resounding conclusions that are reached; scenarios are carefully planned so that all can take a share in the action; themes are remarkable not for themselves but as material for five- or two-fold discussion.

In the Quintet, Arnold shows his skill in games of musical consequences. The unassuming first theme of the first movement yields four distinct motives for debate, variation and expansion:

Ex. 1

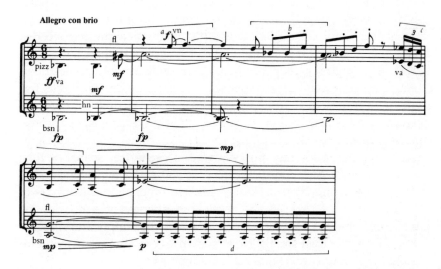

A three-note descending motive (F–E–B flat) provides all the melodic material for the slow movement, the B flat regularly conflicting with the persistent A of a rhythmic ostinato which sounds almost non-stop throughout. It is not until the third movement (3/8 *Allegretto con molto espressivo*) that we meet, after preparatory skirmishes, a regular eight-bar theme of Dvořákian character which is given in turn to every instrument except viola. As in Dvořák's music, the aptness of scoring counts for as much as the themes themselves; the simple but delightful scoring of the second theme of the movement is shown below:

Ex.2

In the Duo, instruments converse on equal terms, the flute's natural vivacity curbed in deference to the more reticent viola. In the opening 3/4 *Andante quasi allegretto* the flute leads off with a serene C major theme, and is soon borrowing the viola's opening scale and working it into the melody. We are led easily on, as in amicable, unhurried conversation which might be described as desultory, if it were not punctuated by a recurrent mournful cadential phrase, which casts a faint shadow over the prevailing C major tonality:

Ex.3

In the vigorous second movement (2/4 *Allegro*) the partners debate an upward-leaping motive of a type we will often meet in later works. Arnold shows himself to be not in the least embarrassed by the limitations of the medium. Clear and economical draughtsmanship ensures that there is no sense of making-do or contrivance while frequent solo and unison passages provide relief from two-voiced chatter.

The last movement opens with a regular and catchy tune (the first in the work) which is at once repeated, but thereafter never makes another complete appearance. Other less symmetrical themes follow and are playfully handled, the descending minor third and the descending scale figures of the first movement working their way into the dialogue from time to time, until both instruments decide, quietly, that it is time to call a halt.

These early works with their many thematic cross-connections are far too innerly coherent to be described as formless, but their forms seem to have evolved, almost casually, in the process of composition. The Violin and Viola Sonatas of 1947 are altogether more weighty, closely structured, and dramatic. The new tone of voice is at once apparent in the very first bars of the Sonata No. 1 for Violin and Piano Op. 15:

Ex.4a

Ex.4b

Arnold at once gets down to business with the simultaneous statement of two energetic themes, **Ex. 4a**. Spare textures, angular and dissonant counterpoints, clearly stated but continually shifting tonalities, suggestions of bitonality and the purposeful movement of basses (which rarely support the expected superstructures) all point to Hindemithian influence. Arnold's resourcefulness in motivic development is made clear even in this short opening sentence; the condensed version of the violin's opening theme is already borrowing x from the piano's second bar, **Ex. 4b** The *gruppetto* figure of bar 4 is soon to be developed in a short episode in which it combines with a rocking accompaniment figure thrown up by the piano in the ninth bar of the movement. There are two independent episodes in which *staccato* piano and *pizzicato* violin play imitative games, and no recapitulation; though the *gruppetto* figure and rocking accompaniment do return in an extended coda.

In the 3/4 *Andante tranquillo* the violin sings a serene G major tune over a rhythmically patterned piano accompaniment, diverging into the minor before resuming the first strain of the melody. As the theme reaches a point of rest, the hitherto subservient piano breaks in *fortissimo* with a furious and dissonant protest in one of the harshest passages Arnold can ever have written, after which the matter and mood of the opening theme are quietly resumed.

Here, for the first time, we catch a glimpse of the darker side of Arnold's character. From one viewpoint, the disturbance can be interpreted as a conflict between partners, the piano rebelling against its servitude. But such abrupt interruptions of an almost too beautiful mood recur too often in Arnold's music to be explained merely as considered acts of musico-dramatic policy. In this case, however, the storm is of short duration and the clouds quickly clear and do not return.

The final 6/8 *Allegro vivace* opens with a characteristic upward-aspiring Arnold theme which is developed by both instruments, roles being freely exchanged. A more sententious tune in double-stopping for violin is repeated by piano, then quickly hustled out of the way, making only furtive appearances thereafter. Later, a tarantella-like rhythm appears in the piano part. This is to play a dominant role in the *Presto* coda, where both instruments with Beethoven-like persistence affirm their own rhythms and tonalities before coming to a last-minute agreement on unison B flat.

The opening *Andante* of the Sonata for Viola and Piano Op. 17 is one of many movements of this period that cannot be analysed by any sort of established rule. (Even Arnold's comparatively simple A–B–A movements, of which there are a fair number, generally contain some formal surprises.) It starts with a long-term canon, the piano imitating the viola at eight bars' distance:

Ex. 5a

Ex. 5b

	1–8	9–10	17–24	24–32
va	A	B	C	D
pno		A	B	C

As the smooth melodic line of the opening eight bars gives way, first to a widely leaping theme in dotted rhythm, then to continuous semiquavers, then to strongly accented *gruppetto* figures in double-stopping, there is a steady build-up of tension and complexity, as shown diagrammatically in **Ex. 5b**. Fresh material appears in the more rhetorical second section, which leads to a sombre *Adagio* (mysterious glissandos in artificial harmonics) and to a varied return of the canonic opening.

In the slow movement, the character of the viola itself rather than the actions and interactions of themes becomes the true subject of the music. The meditative, forlorn aspects of its character are perfectly caught as it sings its long-sustained melodies first quietly in upper registers, then more sonorously on C and G strings. The piano, in the same mood of quietude, contributes a few supporting ideas and rhythms of its own.

The finale is another unorthodox movement, virtually athematic and with no regular developments. After a furious outburst of scales and repeated-note figures, forward movement is suddenly halted by a fragment of a ghostly march. Viola and piano return to the *moto perpetuo* style of the opening; then the pace slackens and the viola harks back to the sombre first-movement *Adagio* before it is cut short by a three-bar *Prestissimo* which brings movement and work to an abrupt end.

In 1963 Arnold told Murray Schafer that he thought his String Quartet No. 1 Op. 23 (written in 1949) was the best work he had yet written. It is easy to understand why he should have been proud of such a closely argued, concentrated, and idiomatic piece. The first movement bears many signs of Bartók's influence: in obsessive use of canon and imitation, in the compactness of its themes, in uncharacteristically close and full textures (in the movement's ninety-seven bars, there are only sixteen in which all four instruments are not simultaneously involved). More specifically, the use of *pizzicato* glissando, glissando harmonics, *pizzicato* chords spread upwards and downwards, suggest that Arnold was very much on the Bartók wavelength.

The three short motives heard in the first bars, **Ex. 6a**, and a falling-third theme provide almost all the material for the first movement and are woven together in complex and ingenious patterns with much imitative writing and little relaxation of tension. **Ex. 6b** shows one such passage, in which a motive derived from x and y is worked in close canon on the two violins. The cello is given an augmented version of the same motive, while the viola sings an extended tune derived from the same source. This episode, the culmination of much contrapuntal dialogue, occurs at the midpoint of the movement, after which a ferocious passage in hammered octaves leads back to a free recapitulation of earlier material.

Ex.6a

Ex.6b

The second movement (2/4 *Vivace*) is one of Arnold's most brilliant and effective scherzos: a lively *moto perpetuo* from which emerges a powerful *legato* theme on lower strings, a later variant being set against *fortissimo pizzicato* chords. The third (6/8 *Andante*) is gentle, lyrical and concerned largely with the implications of the viola's sombre opening theme:

Ex.7

Note the extension by inversion in the third and fourth bars and the ambiguity of the supporting harmonies. Arnold's bitonality is rarely systematic; it is generally used, as here, to cast doubt on an established tonality rather than to create tension between harmonic poles. The music passes from one harmonic ambiguity to another; after a short interlude in which a more rhetorical theme is declaimed against trills by solo or paired instruments, the opening theme returns on viola, and the movement ends, as it began, in B minor.

The last movement (3/4 *Allegro con spirito*) opens with a syncopated, upward-leaping theme which is soon subjected to inversion, imitation, rhythmic transformation, and eventually to fuguing. A contrasting *legato* theme that appears early in the movement is assimilated into the fugue subject, while another episode based on interplay of thirds later returns to bring the work to a peaceful conclusion. This last movement is as ingenious in thematic manipulation as the first, but the themes seem to have sacrificed character in the interest of manoeuvrability; the *legato* tune's main reason for existing seems to be that it should be swallowed up in the fugue. After the dramatic power of the first, the energy and brilliance of the second, and the melodic charm and subtlety of the third movement, we may well feel a little let down by this conclusion. A deliberate lowering of emotional tension, perhaps preluding a return to the everyday world? Or could it be that Arnold simply ran out of steam, or even lost interest, and fell back on craftsmanship to bring matters to a plausible conclusion?

The Sonatinas for Flute, Oboe, Clarinet and Recorder of 1946-52 are designed to delight and divert players as well as listeners, and abound in song-like themes placed in the instruments' 'best' (because most colourful and expressive) registers. They are less contrapuntal and less dissonant than the 'severe' chamber works, and spring fewer formal surprises, many being in straightforward A–B–A forms. The Sonatina for Flute and Piano Op. 19 has special significance in Arnold's development. Arnold had used popular material before, notably in the Shanties; but this is the first time he has mixed polite and popular idioms in the same work. Song-like first movement and chromatic passacaglia are succeeded by a wickedly simple *Allegretto languido*, nothing more than endless repetitions of a single catchy phrase accompanied by the plainest tonic–dominant–supertonic harmonies. Once one has heard the complete work one can imagine no other possible conclusion; but courage was surely needed for Arnold to put his name to music of such total and perfect innocence.

Several of the Sonatinas are studies of the characters of their first performers as well as being, more generally, studies of instrumental character. The calm classic style of Richard Adeney is reflected in the Flute Sonatina, Leon Goossens's finesse in florid passage-work and his ability to melt the heart with some ravishing inflexion of a lyrical theme in the Sonatina for Oboe, Frederick Thurston's robust and dramatic approach in the Clarinet Sonatina. A comparison of the opening paragraphs of the three first Sonatinas will explain better than words the skill with which Arnold catches the character of individual instruments and the quality and variety of his melodic invention:

Ex.8a   Sonatina for Flute

Ex.8b   Sonatina for Oboe

Ex.8c   Sonatina for Clarinet

Though piano keeps a lower profile in the Sonatinas than in the Violin and Viola Sonatas, its dramatic role is still important. It is often the piano's business to question the lyrical mood of the soloist with more agitated rhetoric. In the Clarinet Sonatina the piano evolves its own rhythmic motives from the syncopated chords that punctuate the clarinet's energetic themes; in the last movement of the Oboe Sonatina, the piano counterpoints the oboe's tarantella-like tune with a hunting-horn figure that gives the whole movement an open-air character.

The Divertimento for Wind Trio (flute, oboe, clarinet) Op. 37 of 1952 is more compact than even the shortest of the Sonatinas. A series of six tiny movements, each with its own sharply defined character. Witty, epigrammatic, with just a touch of parody: of the clarinet's rhetorical tendencies in the second, of the learned contrapuntal style in the third. The fifth movement is a march: *Pomp and Circumstance* in miniature, interspersed with arpeggios of ever-increasing brilliance. Once again, as in the Shanties, there is a tiny central movement of lyrical charm and simplicity, in which the oboe sings a quiet and expressive song over a rocking tonic–dominant bass.

The Symphony for Strings Op. 13 was written for the Riddick Orchestra, which gave the first performance in April 1947. This is a virtuoso work, containing some of the most exacting string writing to be found anywhere in Arnold's music. The first movement (4/4 *Allegro ma non troppo*) is vigorous and rhetorical, its use of repeated-note figures suggesting a link with Elgar and the most famous of English virtuoso works for strings, the *Introduction and Allegro*. The opening theme, unusually for Arnold, is made up of several contrasted elements, in the manner of the first theme of Elgar's *Cockaigne* overture.) Several freely rhapsodic themes are ingeniously developed and varied, a twelve-tone row makes two brief and unobtrusive appearances. After having rushed us through much varied musical scenery in the first movement, Arnold now offers rest in a subdued 3/4 *Andantino quasi allegretto*, concerned largely with scalic figures, led by violas and ending with a viola solo – throughout his career, Arnold has generally favoured the veiled and melancholy viola rather than more overtly emotional violin or cello in slow and expressive solos. The third movement is a lively 6/8 *Allegro feroce* with a striking central episode of *sotto voce* musings interrupted by sudden *fortissimos*. This is an accomplished and brilliant work; all that one misses in it is the flavour of the quintessential Arnold.

Concertos

The Concerto No. 1 for Horn and Orchestra Op. 11, Arnold's first concerto for any instrument, was completed in 1945, Dennis Brain giving the first performance in 1946. It is the longest and most expansive of all the concertos, and the only one to contain extended *tuttis* of the traditional variety, in which the orchestra from time to time elbows the soloist aside to show what it can make of the main themes. In a wind instrument concerto long *tuttis* also have practical use, giving the player time to recover breath and lip, and may be welcome to the listener as well, the risk of monotony being greater than in a concerto for violin or piano. Here, however, we sometimes get the impression (not uncommon in virtuoso concertos) that the orchestra is working away diligently at the main themes with no particular dramatic or musical end in view. There are plenty of discursive works in which Arnold takes time off from the main thematic issues to explore melodic byways. Here, for once, there are moments when he seems to be taking his main themes too seriously, and to be plugging the gaps between solo entries with manufactured music.

There are, all the same, many fine things in the Concerto. The first movement (4/4 *Allegro comodo*) opens with a bold and expansive theme which could easily have been written for the old open horn. The more restrained *legato* tune that follows effectively displays another aspect of horn character, but is not in itself of strong individuality, while there is a touch of the study book in some of the brilliant arpeggio passages later in the movement.

In the atmospheric second movement (3/4 *Andante con moto*) the horn ruminates, elaborating on short melodic phrases, often over static harmony or persistent tonic–dominant ostinatos. A touch of unease is provided by the persistent semitonal clashes of muted violins – scoring is so spare and discreet that every note tells. In one very striking passage, the piccolo in low register duets with the soloist – the first example in Arnold's music of an expressive solo for an instrument he has always handled with imagination.

The orchestra introduces both main themes of the last movement (6/8 *Allegro con brio*) in its opening *tutti*. The horn takes up the first of these quietly and in *legato*, making magic out of the slurred rising octave c – c", ideally placed in the best part of the register. There is much lively *détaché* triplet passage-work in all registers (Arnold takes the horn down to an optional A_1), and a long development passage based on a three-note ostinato, in which, as in *Beckus*, Arnold boldly dispenses with all secondary or 'filling-in' voices. The movement ends peacefully, the horn meditating on the *legato* theme as the pace slackens and orchestra quietly affirms the home key of F major.

The Concerto for Clarinet and Strings, completed early in 1948 and first performed by Frederick Thurston, is composed mainly in the more astringent contrapuntal style of the earlier sonatas, but finds room for one catchy tune in the first movement. The clarinet is in rhetorical mood, its wide-ranging themes suave and heroic by turns, leaping rapidly from register to register or dazzling with brilliant scales and arpeggios. Arnold later overcame any inhibitions he may have had concerning the inclusion in 'serious' works of tunes in popular idioms; but here he seems to be apologizing for the catchy tune of the first movement, playing around during the development section with a short repeated-note figure from its first bar as though hoping to raise its status by giving it an honest job of work to do.

A dramatic recitative which introduces the slow movement is twice echoed at later stages, functioning as a sort of ritornello. In the central section, an aspiring theme (a near relation of the opening motive of the String Symphony) is ingeniously worked in close imitations. The 6/8 *Allegro con fuoco* is a movement of the same type as the finale of the String Symphony; equally energetic and equally resourceful in maintaining impetus. But there are no great revelations of instrumental character, no tunes that make us catch our breath in wonder.

Arnold had perhaps reached the dangerous stage when a composer can turn out music that 'works' to order, whether or not he has anything particular to say. Maybe too the playing of Frederick Thurston spoke less eloquently to him than that of Benny Goodman, for whom, nearly a quarter of a century later, the Second Concerto was written. The combination of clarinet and strings may have been in itself less stimulating than the rarer combination of the Concerto for Piano Duet and Strings Op. 32, which Arnold wrote in 1951 at the instigation of Mosco Carner. Helen Pyke and Paul Hamburger broadcast the work in 1951 and later performed it at the Proms in 1953.

Arnold had no special love for the piano as solo instrument. Like Hindemith and Vaughan Williams, he generally treats it as an instrument-of-all-work, a bearer of harmonic and melodic messages, showing little interest in 'pianistic' devices, figurations, effects obtainable by spacing, pedalling, and the various sorts of finger magic, which virtuosi specialize. But his use of the piano in this Concerto, in a limited role – often almost as an instrument of tuned percussion – is unfailingly apt. Even the somewhat brutal and densely chorded dialogue between the players in two of the central variations of the slow movement is appropriate enough in context.

The Concerto is tightly and clearly structured, with two light and entertaining movements enclosing a weighty passacaglia. The chattering first movement rouses memories of the lighter-hearted French piano works of the twenties. Interest lies in textures rather than in themes, with the pianists playing a *concertante* role, elaborating and adorning the simple melodic formula that provides most of the material, and which appears augmented in a more tranquil central section. The *Larghetto* is based on a seven-bar theme, and builds up from dark and mysterious beginnings through nine clearly differentiated variations of growing elaboration and intensity. Tension is released in an extended dance-like variation before the first two variations return in reverse order – a good example of Arnold's resourcefulness in bending a conventional form to his own uses. The finale is a robust 6/8, enlivened by many strongly stressed cross-rhythms and with a grotesque chromatic second theme that owes something to pop music, something to Bartók:

Ex. 9

The oboe appears in much the same character in the Concerto for Oboe and Strings Op. 39 (completed in 1952) as in the earlier Sonatina; which is not so surprising when we know that it too was written for Leon Goossens, who gave the first performance at the Royal Festival Hall, London, in June 1953. The first movement of the Concerto, like that of the Sonatina, opens with an almost unbroken span of oboe melody (4/4 *Cantabile*) that takes us more than halfway through the movement; themes are closely interwoven, or shared between soloist and orchestra in contrapuntal dialogue, the song-like mood broken only by a brief and dramatic dotted-rhythm episode for strings alone which precedes the recapitulation.

The second movement is one of Arnold's fleet 6/8 scherzos and a near relation of the finale of the Sonatina; a free rondo in the form of a multi-decker sandwich with layers of varying thickness. Tonality in both movements is ambiguous, the first making play with modulating themes that continually tease us with the prospect of a cadence only to lead us to another doubtful harmonic crossroads, while in the second the conflict between E minor and E flat minor of the first bars is immediately echoed in the main theme, which veers between the same two keys. (Similar processes are at work in the last movement of the Serenade for Small Orchestra.)

The third movement opens with a staid and formal eight–bar minuet tune, many times repeated with varied counterpoints. A second span of melody is equally well designed to display the player's refined *pianissimos* and needle-sharp articulation; but we seem to have entered a smaller world of music, in which manners and good breeding count for more than warm-hearted, spontaneous communication. The soloist signs off quietly, refusing to make an exhibition of himself in characteristic last-movement fashion. But the effect is a little disconcerting – rather as though an acquaintance who had expansively confided his most intimate and tender feelings to us was suddenly to regret his indiscretion and to withdraw behind a screen of polite formalities.

The Serenade Op. 26 is designated 'for Small Orchestra' rather than 'for Chamber Orchestra'; a significant distinction, in view of the fact that woodwind, brass (two each of horns and trumpets), timpani and strings appear in their traditional orchestral roles rather than in more fluid chamber-music relationship. The Serenade is none the less conceived precisely in terms of the reduced forces used. This is one of the most delightful of Arnold's lighter works: buoyant in mood, simple in structure, euphonious, scored lightly and luminously, a rich storehouse of tunes lively, radiant, and serene. As in the Sonatinas, harmonies that are often quietly subversive rather than perverse or contradictory allow us to view apparently simple diatonic tunes in strange perspective.

Each of the three short movements is very much all-of-a-piece, establishing and sustaining its own mood. The second is a simple, song-like movement with few complexities. The first and third movements are unified by unobtrusive interconnections between themes, and between themes and accompaniments. Thus, in the opening *Allegretto*, the accompaniment figure of the opening bars is picked up in the fifth bar of the life-affirming theme (a close relation of an important theme in the Second Symphony) which soon sails in on the violins, while the third-based motive of the central section (**Ex. 10c**) returns in a decorative role when the first theme is recapitulated towards the end of the movement:

Ex.10a

Ex.10b

Ex.10c

In the last movement, the seventh chords of the brass's preliminary call to action foreshadow the tonal conflict that is to follow as G major themes are questioned by persistent F sharp minor harmonies, and later, as the solo trumpet spells out the conflicting harmonies melodically in an exhilarating solo:

Ex.11a

Ex.11b

Not for the first time, Arnold saves one powerful theme until late in the movement.

The Smoke (slang for 'London') is dedicated to the Bournemouth Municipal Orchestra and Rudolf Schwarz, who first performed it in 1948. *A Sussex Overture* (1951) was written for Herbert Menges's Southern Philharmonic Orchestra and first heard in Brighton. The two overtures have features in common. Both are vigorous, robust, cast in a familiar popular-overture mould. A brilliant and colourful opening *tutti* causes the audience to sit up and take notice. Broad and more songful themes follow; excitement is then whipped up and each overture ends with an imposing peroration for full orchestra and a return of the big tune. *A Sussex Overture*, the more interesting of the two, is a sustained and resourceful scherzo in which the 6/8 metre of the opening *Allegro con brio* is maintained throughout the overture's eight-minute length. There are happy incidental inventions in the scoring, ingenious workings of the main motives in ostinato and in canon. The weak spot of both works lies in the big tunes, which are not among Arnold's best. Both return untransformed, though in grandiose orchestral dress, in the final pages, and hardly seem to deserve such VIP treatment.

By contrast, the tunes of the two sets of *English Dances* Op. 27 and 33 of 1950 and 1951 fulfil their destinies in the most satisfying ways. These were written in response to a request from Arnold's publisher, Lengnick, who suggested to several composers that they should provide English companions for Dvořák's *Slavonic Dances*. Arnold was the only one to respond, characteristically supplying a double helping of dances. It would be hard to trace the provenance of his dance tunes, which avoid all suggestion of folky modality, but which are still very much in an English tradition. The first of the second set, indeed, is almost a paraphrase of the Quaker tune that appears in Aaron Copland's *Appalachian Spring*. One or two others resemble the 'manufactured' dance tunes that appear in Playford's *The English Dancing Master* and other seventeenth–and eighteenth–century collections.

As in so many Arnold works, it is not so much (or not only) the tunes that make for the success (artistic as well as commercial) of the *Dances*. Happily devised accompaniment figures, varied orchestration, and the well-judged planning of the two sequences are just as important – as one realizes when one hears dances extracted from the sequences (the first dance of the second set, which forms an appropriately attention-catching overture to the second set, sounds merely rowdy when it appears on its own in 'Richard Baker's Dozen' or some similar collection of truncated masterworks). There is the same unobtrusive transference of material from themes to accompaniment figures and vice versa that we meet in the chamber works; varied formal schemes, tunes that parse oddly into uneven phrase-lengths, and occasionally quite surprising harmonizations of straightforwardly diatonic tunes. But abnormalities are presented against a background of normality; Arnold sets out to delight rather than to mystify or to show off his composerly skills. Here as elsewhere, he proves that he can afford to take on board familiar and well-used melodic and harmonic formulae because he has the bailast of individuality needed to transform them for his own purposes.

The Symphonic Study: *Machines* Op. 30, though not published until 1984, derives from a ten-minute score written in 1951 for the documentary film *Report on Steel*. Scored for strings, brass and percussion, it consists of a terse set of five variations on three short figures which appear in the opening bars. The variations are textural rather than melodic or harmonic, the main motives recurring regularly in clearly recognizable forms and also supplying the material for many subsidiary figurations.

Ex.12

hns & perc. omitted

Only the third variation, in which violins take off in sustained melodic flights, moves far from its thematic origins. Tempi are mostly brisk; implacably repeated ostinatos establish the mechanical connection. *Machines*, as one might expect from its subject and origins, is a fairly impersonal work, but well designed to display the sonority and athletic prowess of a virtuoso orchestra *minus* its woodwind section.

4

SYMPHONIC LANDMARKS
First and Second Symphonies

The First and Second Symphonies deserve a chapter to themselves by reason of their individual merits and because they form important landmarks in Arnold's early career. In the First, he proved his ability to speak in the bold and plain terms appropriate to a big 'public' work and to use his basic material consistently, cogently, and economically, sticking firmly to the main issues. The tone of voice is objective; Arnold seems to be flexing his symphonic muscles, proving to the world and to himself that he is capable of great things. The first movement in particular resembles functional architecture which makes a virtue of severity, scorning the arts of embellishment that attempt to conceal structure behind decorative cladding.

The Second, by contrast, is both lyrical and (in the finale) dance-inspired. One could be likened to muscular prose, the other to lyric poetry – which is not to imply that the First is prosaic, the Second meandering or rhapsodic; it is in fact as clearly structured as any classical symphony. Arnold has discovered, in the four years that have passed since the composition of the First, that the writing of a symphony could be a joyful as well as a solemn duty. The lighter, airier mood of the Second is reflected in the orchestration. Arnold had refined his skills, learning to blend and contrast instrumental timbres with Mahlerian subtlety and imagination, so that the boundaries between orchestral and chamber-music idioms are often blurred.

Symphony No. 1 Op. 22

Except in the case of a few strictly serial works, claims that the course of a whole movement is somehow decided or predestined in the opening bars (or even chords) are hardly ever to be taken seriously. But it would be true to say that motives or figures derived from the first three bars of Arnold's first portentous unison, **Ex. 1a**, pervade the first movement. The figure **b** is already augmented in the fourth and fifth bars, with a final emphatic reiteration of a_2 symmetrically balancing the rising tone of the first bar. **Ex. 1b** shows some of the ways in which key figures are deployed in every bar from 13 to 29, the ascending major second, a_1, its inversion, a_2, and the minor-third figure in **b** giving rise to a developing sequence of thematic extensions, transformations, and ostinatos:

Ex. 1a

Ex. 1b

(continued)

A more lyrical theme in F major which appears at bar 138 (just after letter J) brings a change of mood; but the background chords still remind us of the rising and falling tones **a₁** and **a₂**:

Ex.2

Neither the sombre and dramatic development nor the recapitulation introduce much fresh material. **Ex. 1a** appears in a new light at the beginning of the recapitulation when it returns quietly in B minor on woodwind and harp before the tonality swings back to D minor, while the lyrical second theme reappears *fortissimo* on strings and woodwind (again in F major), now set against the rhythmic figure **a₃** on brass (see **Ex. 1b**). The movement ends without ceremony with abrupt reference to the opening master theme:

Ex.3

If pushed to say what the first movement is 'about', one might suggest that it is concerned largely with frustrated attempts to break free from the restrictions imposed by the opening motive, which denies or cuts short aspiring melodies or gentler, reflective interludes. The central *Andantino*, which provides a sort of buffer between the two vigorous and active outer movements, is by contrast as quiet and unassuming as one of Sibelius's gentler intermezzo movements:

Ex.4

Two brief but shocking interruptions involving brass and percussion serve only to emphasize the first theme's contemplative character. There is little in the way of motivic development; but imaginative instrumentation ensures that the main theme appears in many lights. The handling of the full orchestra in *pianissimo*; expressive uses of the solo piccolo and bassoon (taken to *Rite of Spring* heights), close-spaced harp chords in lowest registers are all worth noting. In Arnold, as in Shostakovich, colour, texture, spacing, use of 'normal' or extreme registers, are often as much *of the essence* as motivic and harmonic developments.

The last movement opens with a lively fugal theme for unison violins, followed in turn by woodwind, horns, and basses:

Ex.5

Imitative counter-themes are freely contrapuntal, and Arnold soon confirms that he has no intention of playing the game by strict academic rules. When trombones and trumpets take over the theme, Arnold uses the Verdian device of punctuating his fugue with emphatic *staccato* chords (even so, at the first performance at the

Cheltenham Festival in 1951, the *Times* critic ignored this precedent and censured Arnold for his inability to write a proper fugue). This movement, unlike the first two, is rich in subsidiary themes; one rising third figure suggests possible back references to both first and second movements but thematic connections in Arnold's music are generally so explicitly clear that the resemblance may well be coincidental. There are regularly patterned episodes for contrasted instrumental groups, two further mock-expositions, the first for wood wind, the second (inverted) for strings, and a free recapitulation of earlier episodic material. The last *fortissimo* episode culminates in triumphant fanfares and the transformation of the fugal subject to a lively 2/4 march theme:

Ex.6

After a dramatic pause the main theme appears in a final transformation, *Maestoso* 3/2, over a bass of the sort that, since Stravinsky's *Symphony of Psalms*, has regularly been described as 'hieratic':

Ex.7

The Symphony as a whole turns out to be not quite the work of massive proportions, leisurely and far-reaching developments, that the imposing Euston Arch of an opening leads us to expect. Neither the compact first movement nor the finale with its three fugal expositions and ingenious transformations quite sustains the epic vein. The opening theme perhaps proved too weighty to be easily manipulable, too limited and definite in character to lend itself to symphonic manoeuvre. Certainly the imposing signing-off process at the end of the third movement is appropriate to an epic; but the jauntiness of the transformed fugue subject suggests that Arnold himself doesn't take his grand peroration too seriously, and may even be deliberately questioning the validity of the epic species.

Symphony No. 2 Op. 40

An arresting opening gesture heralds the threefold statement of the main theme of the opening *Allegretto*. The first two statements, and the opening of the third, are shown here, to illustrate the way in which the opening motive, **x**, is used as a punctuation mark between sentences, and also to give an indication of the transparent chamber-music orchestration that is one of the most delightful and refreshing characteristics of the movement. More than half of the movement (on a bar count) is taken up with restatements of this theme or its head phrase:

Ex.8

(*continued*)

A modulating transition passage, **Ex. 9a**, leads to the second main theme, **Ex. 9b**, which will reappear in the recapitulation but which plays no part in the development:

The movement is in uncomplicated sonata form, with clearly defined first and second subjects in E flat and A (both recapitulated in E flat). The tonality of the opening tune, so clearly outlined in the first almost unaccompanied statement, is never questioned; when the theme at last appears on the full orchestra, at the beginning of the recapitulation, it is supported throughout its course by plainest E flat major harmony.

Coherence is ensured (as in many of Arnold's lyrical movements) by unobtrusively established references and cross-connections. The sharp and emphatic chords and answering phrase for timpani and basses shown at **x** in **Ex. 8** continue to serve in varied forms as punctuation points or markers. The next example shows a characteristic process of transformation: **x** appears (soon after letter D in the miniature score) in the background to the second main theme, **Ex.10a** is reduced to a rhythm when the same tune is repeated, **Ex. 10b**; then expanded in a figure which is also reminiscent of figure **y** in the transition theme, **Ex. 10c**. Simultaneously, a solemn augmentation of the head motive of **Ex. 8** appears on the brass in a passage that springs so naturally from what has gone before that its thematic origins could well pass unnoticed:

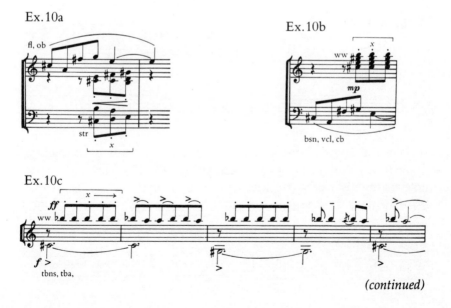

Ex.10a

Ex.10b

Ex.10c

(continued)

The 6/8 scherzo, cast in A–B–A form, bears a family resemblance to other fleet-footed Arnold scherzos, with a touch of the grotesquerie of *Beckus*. A number of the short themes which are at first handed around the orchestra are derived from the opening horn chords:

Ex.11a

Ex.11b

Ex.11c

A bold and angular theme next emerges which ends by plunging dramatically down through four octaves in a series of seventh leaps; note the family resemblance between x and the head motive of the main theme of the first movement:

Ex.12

In the central section, scampering exchanges between strings and woodwind, *pianissimo e staccato,* are roughly interrupted by brass and percussion. After an abbreviated recapitulation, in which the angular theme of **Ex. 12** appears *fortissimo* in full orchestral dress, the movement ends with a final assertion of **x**.

The *Lento* opens with a threefold statement of a vagrant and mournful theme given first to bassoon, then violas, then oboe (all instruments specializing in pathos), while tenuous background harmonies shift uncertainly before veering towards B minor:

Ex.13

(continued)

A radiant motive in E major now offers consolation – note the effective use of the full orchestra in *pianissimo*. The rise from fifth to major third, once more echoes the head motive of the main theme of the first movement:

Ex.14

The new theme recedes into the background and is later reduced to a monotonic rhythm. **Ex. 13** returns to its way through the orchestra; an impassioned climax for strings and brilliant brass fanfares follows (letter K); the dotted-note rhythm of these fanfares is incorporated into a new woodwind counter-theme which combines with **Ex. 14** over a long-sustained pedal:

Ex.15

After further searching developments we return at last to E major and to the theme of consolation. But there is no more than a glimpse of peace and content before the opening theme returns at its original pitch (solo horn) and resignedly settles for B minor.

Mood and key change abruptly as the final *Allegro con brio* launches, after eleven bars' prelude, into a robust A–B–A dance tune in E flat, from the same stable as the second of the *English Dances* (Set 1) but with an extra rhythmic twist in the tail of the first A section:

Ex.16

Unison horns announce a new theme, followed fugue-wise by trumpets and trombones. Heavy string chords punctuate the fugal development (another fugue with a difference):

Ex.17

(continued)

*E unison on full orchestra

The contours of the new theme suggest a connection with the mournful theme of the slow movement; and in fact, it plays a similar role, casting a shadow over the optimistic mood engendered by its sister theme. A brief return of the dance tune leads to a curious episode in which the piccolo takes over **Ex. 18** against an eerie background of string harmonics and scale fragments on xylophone and flutes:

Ex.18

A new episode develops from these fragmented scales, after which bassoon, then upper strings, ruminate on **Ex. 17** over a persistent side-drum rhythm, and long-sustained pedal E. The movement side-slips back into E flat and the dance tune returns for the last time, to be followed by a short *Lento molto e maestoso* coda.

We talk too lightly of masterworks; and certainly if it is necessary for a masterwork to be deep, portentous, remarkable for technical or formal innovations, Arnold's Second Symphony hardly fills the bill. Yet if a 'masterwork' is a piece in which one can hardly imagine a passage or note changed for the better, then this Symphony surely qualifies. Its four movements complement one another admirably. There is no ostentatious flexing of intellectual muscle, no striking of histrionic attitudes, but a constant flow of lively and apt musical invention. There is just enough doubt and darkness to make us properly appreciative of the sunlight, the buoyancy, the lyricism, the humour, the radiant good spirits which are so special to this Symphony, and so rarely found in 'serious' works of the period. In this sense, the Second Symphony is a startlingly original work; free of mystification, free of *Angst*; one that none of Arnold's contemporaries could have written, or would have thought of writing, even if they had been bold enough to flout the 'spirit of the age' so outrageously. Its production marked a sort of musical coming of age for Arnold; he had attained the technical means, the self-knowledge and the self-confidence to write a major work that was entirely his own.

5

COMPOSER AS ILLUSTRATOR
Film Music

In film, the composer's job is to support the work of others rather than to strike out on his own. Occasionally, music plays as important a role as the illustrations in a children's picture book, without which the story would lose all colour and interest. But there is still some truth in the often-repeated generalization that the best film music is inaudible. As Georges Auric once wrote: 'We do not go to the cinema to hear music. We require it to deepen and prolong in us the screen's visual impressions.'

Despite this, there is never a shortage of composers eager to write for film. Financial rewards aside, any young composer welcomes the chance to use large resources, to have his music played by professionals, with the assurance that it will be heard (if not listened to) by large audiences. Writing for film or theatre allows him to get out of his own skin, to feed on the vision and inspiration of creators in other fields, instead of having to spin music spider-like out of his own entrails. A film composer, moreover, has a degree of anonymity which enables him to write with a freedom denied to him (or which he denies himself) in the concert hall. He can try out this or that manner of writing without being accused of self-betrayal; he has the chance to experiment without having to live for ever with the fruits of his experiments.

There are some for whom such work, at least when undertaken on the grand scale, represents a form of prostitution. Many others have managed to adapt to the specialized demands of the medium without compromising their standards or losing their own characters in the process. A few – Copland, Prokofiev, Henze, and Arnold among them – have even discovered new aspects of their own characters in the process.

In Arnold's case, film work seems to have awakened a dramatic instinct that might otherwise have lain dormant. Particularly when co-operating with directors of the first rank, he found in film the extra-musical inspiration that tended to elude him in the setting of words. And even in the case of a composer as experienced in the use of the orchestra as Arnold, there was much to be learned in the process of writing score after score for the best players in London, often hearing his music played almost before the ink was dry.

Being highly practical, a master of many styles, having the confidence and resilience essential for all those who enter the film jungle, he was well equipped for the work. He was also the quickest of quick workers (the thirty-four-minute score of *The Bridge on the River Kwai* was turned out in less than three weeks). He knew what could and could not be expected of a studio orchestra in the limited rehearsal time available, and was familiar with the various tricks of the trade – thus, he would regularly write doubling parts for all woodwind (every flautist also required to play piccolo, and so on) knowing that the best performers would be attracted by the doubling fees involved.

As a craftsman-composer with a living to make, Arnold naturally and willingly tended to conform to studio conventions. Much of the film music is cast in familiar moulds and makes use of well-worn formulae of the genre; it was the uses he made of music, rather than the idioms or syntax of the music itself, or even the speed at which he worked, that confirmed him in his position as one of the most highly valued film composers of his generation.

He wrote his first film score in 1947 (at which time he was still playing principal trumpet with the London Philharmonic Orchestra) supplying fourteen minutes' music for a twenty-four-minute documentary dealing with the work of the Swiss Avalanche Patrol. Four further documentaries followed before, in 1948, he graduated to feature films, composing a twenty-minute score for *Badger's Green*, an hour-long comedy directed by John Irwin. Thereafter the pace quickened. Arnold wrote six further documentary scores in 1948, conducting his own music for *Mining Review* (in later years, he was to conduct many of his own recording sessions). Sixteen scores (including four features) were composed in 1949. In 1952 he produced over three-and-a-half hours' film music for eight feature films and two documentaries. By 1966, he had written the music for 118 films. He composed over thirty-three hours' music for the eighty-one films of which the timings are known; allowing for the untimed thirty-seven, we can calculate that he must have written in all over forty-eight hours' film music – more than twice as much music as Wagner composed for *The Ring*, and considerably more than Ravel wrote during his whole life.

Arnold himself has salvaged a limited amount of film music for use in concert works. The Symphonic Study: *Machines* drew on material from an early documentary, *Report on Steel*. Music from *The Sound Barrier* was worked up into an orchestral Rhapsody. The second of the *Four Scottish Dances* derives directly from the music for the documentary *The Beautiful County of Ayr*. A fragment of folk-like melody in *The Reckoning* was expanded, in the Eighth Symphony, to form the main theme of the first movement. Various 'themes' and 'songs', even 'vocal albums' were published at the time when some of the more popular films were released, and are best ignored by those who want to gauge Arnold's worth as a film composer. They often have little to do with the music as Arnold first wrote it, having been simplified and thrust into new shapes by arrangers, with words of Christmas-cracker standard added to instrumental themes.

For the rest, Arnold's film music can be heard only on the rare occasions when the films are revived on television (often without a composer credit in the advance billing). Considering that Arnold himself has conducted no further rescue operations beside those mentioned above, it might be thought pointless to discuss it at all. But the exercise has some value if it allows us to view the composer in a new perspective; demonstrably the same man, but working to different ends. Film, in spite of the inevitable frustrations and strains involved in the work, took the place of opera in Arnold's life, allowing him to develop and exercise musico-dramatic skills that might otherwise never have been brought into play.

The notes that follow may give some idea of ways in which the work of Arnold the film composer paralleled, complemented, and perhaps enriched the work of the concert composer. My sample includes films from most periods of his film career: a documentary, two comedies, two war films, two romanticized 'true-life' stories, one murderous and sexy drama in the ruthless 1960s manner. Several of these are Arnold's own favourites; others I have chosen because they were made by distinguished directors or seemed likely to reveal Arnold in some previously unfamiliar aspect.

Women in Our Time (1948) was the first of five documentaries in the series *This Modern Age* for which Arnold provided music. Music was almost continuous (Arnold supplied nineteen minutes' music for a twenty-minute film), and was not closely integrated with action or visual imagery, as it had been in a few earlier British documentaries (*Song of Ceylon*, with music by Walter Leigh, *Night Mail* and *Coal Face*, with music by Britten, come to mind). *Women in Our Time*, apart from early newsreel shots of suffragette activities, was informative rather than dramatic, including interviews with distinguished academics and parliamentarians as well as sequences in which women were seen working on farms, in factories or crèches, and so on. Arnold's music, reproduced at such low levels that it is often hard to follow even the melodic line, provides a background tapestry of sound, broadly appropriate to the context – though why anyone should have demanded background music for a scripted interview with Lady Pethick Lawrence is hard to conceive. For title music and outdoor scenes, there is an expansive lyrical theme, which is later transformed and varied in many ways, appearing in waltz time in a scene at the hairdresser's:

Ex. 1

A haunting theme for alto saxophone is first heard as we see women workers cleaning up in London's tube tunnels at night, and reappears later in various contexts:

Ex. 2

Ethel Smyth's 'March of the Suffragettes' makes several appearances; 'Lillibulero' accompanies scenes of army drill, and at one point, for no apparent reason, the theme of the variations of Beethoven's Piano Sonata Op. 106 makes a momentary appearance. What is most impressive about the score is the broad span of the *cantabile* tunes, the resourcefulness with which Arnold keeps going almost non-stop for nineteen minutes, and the freshness and apparent spontaneity of invention – no warmed-up Vaughan Williams for countryside scenes, no spinning out of melodic or harmonic formulae. One's only complaint is that so much of the music is of unnecessarily high quality and interest for the purpose it had to serve; musicians in the audience could well be distracted from the film by some of the adventures which the theme of **Ex. 1** undergoes, while **Ex. 2** rises in its eloquence far above the needs of the occasion.

For *The Sound Barrier* (1952), Arnold provided only twenty-six minutes' music for a two-hour film. (For air sequences, the director David Lean, following the trend of the times, used mostly natural sound.) Terence Rattigan's screenplay wove a fairly flimsy plot around the loves, tragedies, and triumphs of the test pilots, designers and manufacturers involved in the attempts to break through the sound barrier; Ralph Richardson did his best with the part of the autocratic boss of the aircraft firm. Arnold's leading title-music motive **Ex. 3a**, which appears later on in many different guises, manages to be both heroic and threatening. A mournful chromatic figure associated with death is also distantly related to this motive. But the buoyant diatonic theme (**Ex. 3b**) used for 'men at work' scenes, which perhaps typifies the courage, energy and pertinacity of pilots and designers, comes from another world of music:

Ex.3a

Ex.3b

cantabile

In *Hobson's Choice* (1953), the second David Lean film with an Arnold
score, music plays a larger part. Harold Brighouse's north country
comedy (originally a play) tells the story of a shy and gentle
bootmaker (Willie Mossop) whose life changes when his boss's
daughter decides to marry him and make a proper man of him.
Arnold provides the unworldly Willie with a deliberately ungainly
6/8 theme, a slightly old-fashioned sort of 'comedy number' tune
which retains its identity in many transformations:

Ex.4

There are two scenes in which music plays a major role, and in
which Arnold demonstrates his potential as musical dramatist. On
Willie Mossop's marriage night, his bride retires to the bedroom after
a tender love scene, and Willie nervously prepares to follow her. The
love music is of expansive, Straussian splendour, with an eloquent
violin solo of a type that Arnold never allows himself to write in his
concert music – an example of the way in which the film composer
can sometimes free himself from concert-hall inhibitions and become,
for the length of a scene, another man. The music changes to a brisk,
semi-military march as Willie enters the bedroom.

In another scene, Willie's father-in-law and former boss reels home
late at night after drowning his anxieties in drink, staggers round the
town square, is ludicrously bewildered when he sees the moon
reflected in a puddle (shimmering quasi-electronic glissandos), and at

last falls down the barrel chute of a brewery. This provides a great opportunity for Charles Laughton to mime at length, and for Arnold to provide music that not only fits the action but almost seems to dictate it. (In fact, it was composed, as usual, after the film had been cut.) Arnold works the Willie Mossop theme into an extended sequence that shadows every move, the fusion between music and action as complete as in the scene in the third act of Wagner's *Die Meistersinger* in which Beckmesser makes off with Hans Sachs's manuscript.

The Bridge on the River Kwai of 1957 was the last and finest of the David Lean films for which Arnold wrote the music, his score deservedly winning him an Oscar. Arnold provides atmospheric music tinged with Easternism for desperate journeys through the Burmese forests, with a charming pastoral episode when the escaping prisoner finds sanctuary in a Burmese village. He introduces jazz as the music of civilized ease when the scene moves to British headquarters at Ceylon, and transforms a heroic military motive into a love theme when William Holden falls for a Burmese girl.

But the chief fascination of the score lies in the naturalistic incorporation of music into the action. No one who has seen the film is likely to forget the episode in which the prisoners march across the bridge whistling 'Colonel Bogey', or the grotesque camp concert at which British prisoners sing their favourite music-hall songs in the middle of the tropical forest and surrounded by Japanese guards. What fewer may have noticed (and what the audience was never meant to notice) is the unobtrusive skill with which Arnold blends naturalistic and composed elements. How aptly the whistled 'Colonel Bogey' merges into Arnold's own brisk instrumental march, heard at first in counterpoint with it; how, in the final scenes, love music and martial music contend as the mad English colonel (Alec Guinness) walks alone onto the just-completed bridge; how the repeated hoot of the approaching Japanese train sounds as menacingly as Hunding's horn, raising the tension almost to breaking point. Arnold's music is linked so closely to the visual and dramatic context that musical quotation would be meaningless.

In 1958 Arnold wrote the music for another war film, *The Key*, directed by Carol Reed, in which William Holden again starred, joining the British Navy and falling for Sophia Loren. The leading motive of the film, which first appears in the title music, comes from the same stable as the leading motive of *The Sound Barrier* (see **Ex. 4**):

Ex.5a   Ex.5b

Whereas in *The Sound Barrier* the leading motive stood for heroism and death, here the leading motive represents heroism and love – Wagnerian parallels would not be hard to find. A *legato* transformation (**Ex. 5b**) appears in love scenes, fulfilling its function as naturally and convincingly as if freshly inspired rather than the product of manipulation and contrivance. Once again, Arnold refreshes us by introducing several lively and quite independent themes for the less dramatic scenes of action – how often one has been exasperated by film composers who work their leading themes to death in the interests of unity or because their lack of originality forces them to economize on material!

Arnold did not always have the luck to work with directors of the calibre of Lean and Reed. *Value for Money*, directed by Ken Annakin in 1955, is a run-of-the-mill comedy in which a cautious Yorkshire lad falls for a London showgirl (Diana Dors), with three scenes in which music plays a major part. For a long song-and-dance sequence at a London theatre, Arnold writes Noël-Cowardish show music that is virtually indistinguishable from the real thing. There is also an almost poetic scene in which the lovestruck boy, travelling back home on the coach, breaks into a heartfelt northern folk song – another effective piece of musical naturalism. Music is also integrated into the action in a scene in which Diana Dors opens the new municipal swimming pool with the local brass band blaring away untunefully in the background, its appalling performance adding to the frightfulness of the occasion. Arnold takes his tone from the director, and matches the screen situation with a musical joke as unsubtle as the comedy itself.

The Inn of the Sixth Happiness (1958), a nine-reeler directed by Mark Robson, features Ingrid Bergman as Gladys Aylward, the American missionary to China who led an army of children across the mountains to safety after the Japanese invasion. Only natural sounds are used in scenes of violence and terror, music being identified with constructive forces and gentler emotions. There are hints of local colour in the scoring and in the use of gapped scales in the mock-Eastern music, scored for a chamber ensemble including harp and celesta. But the most heard, and most sumptuous tune in the score is pure Arnold – a long, soaring theme, which is expanded into a full-length *Intermezzo* designed to be played during the intermission.

This is another of those tunes that Arnold, with his dread of schmaltz, might have hesitated to dwell on in a concert work; but in the popular-theatrical context it needs no excuse or justification – we may even regret that Arnold did not allow the principal theme of his Fifth Symphony its head in like manner. At the end of the film, the children march down from the mountains lustily singing 'Knick knack paddy whack, give a dog a bone' – the use of naturalistic sound and the effect of cultural disorientation takes one back to that scene in *River Kwai* where the prisoners whistle 'Colonel Bogey' as they march across the bridge. Once again, however unlikely the episode, it's a musico-dramatic image that no one is going to forget.

The Reckoning, director Jack Gold, was Arnold's one-from-last feature film, made in 1969. This is a formula picture (sex, violence, skulduggery in high places the chief ingredients) partly redeemed by Nicol Williamson's fine performance as the ruthless, upwardly mobile hero from humblest Irish-Liverpool origins who is playing for high stakes in the City and is simultaneously involved in a blood feud back home. The title music is based on a forceful, driving theme from the age of Beat. In a later scene, the hero returns to Liverpool to visit his dying father; as he arrives at the family home, we hear, faintly, a snatch of a folk-like theme like the distant memory of an innocent childhood; a striking and moving effect, all the more tantalizing because the theme has vanished again almost before we have heard it.

This is the only appearance in the film of the tune that Arnold was to develop at length in the first movement of his Eighth Symphony, and we never hear it complete. Though the connection declares itself in no obvious manner, the mock folk tune and the driving theme of the title music are thematically related:

Ex. 6a

Ex. 6b

In a later scene, the drunken hero disconcerts the guests at a rowdy London party by breaking into 'Believe me that all those endearing young charms . . .' – as in *Value for Money*, the simple countryman-beneath-the-skin asserts himself when his defences are down. I suspect that these scenes had some special significance for Arnold himself, who in works of this period had arranged so many marriages between 'composed' music and folk-derived or -inspired tunes, and who had personal experience of the dilemmas of those who are transplanted (or who transplant themselves) from one environment to another.

Ballet Music

Though, in ballet, music provides the essential thread on which all synchronized movement depends, it often seems that ballet music, no less than film music, is inaudible to the spectator, and most of all to the confirmed balletomane. Reading through old *Times* reviews of first performances of Arnold's four Covent Garden ballets, we find that the music never gets more than a couple of lines, and that reviewers have not the vaguest notion as to what has been going on in the orchestra pit. In general, few seem to notice that opera orchestras are regularly at their worst on ballet evenings, that after the premiere ballet music is rarely properly rehearsed and that ballet conductors as a species are held in lowest regard by their players.

Yet in this area too, there have been a few impresarios who have treated music as an integral and essential part of the composite work of art, and a few composers (Delibes, Tchaikovsky, Stravinsky, Ravel, Copland, and Bliss among them) of whom one could say that, if you don't know their ballet music, you hardly know them at all. Composing for ballet drew them into new regions of discovery and self-discovery, while experiences gained in the theatre fed back into their work in other fields.

This was hardly the case with Arnold. He had been an enthusiastic ballet-goer in his youth, and from the first moved with familiar ease in the new medium, exploiting its more extravagant conventions with obvious delight. Yet the four original ballets do not form a very significant part of his total output. He has himself said that he prefers writing for the concert hall, producing the sort of music 'he would like to listen to himself'. But the ballet scores have their own special interest. Like film scores, they give us a glimpse of composition processes uncensored by the super-ego; since, by tacit agreement, film and ballet composers are given a holiday from the stern duty of being *true to themselves*. Lastly, there is the intrinsic interest and quality of music which, if it never attempts to reveal the hidden depths of the composer's soul, or to propound any startlingly original propositions, is always apt, tuneful, seductively scored, putting over the dramatic message (when there is a dramatic message) clearly and forcefully.

Arnold's first ballet, *Homage to the Queen* Op. 42, was composed for the Sadler's Wells Theatre Ballet (forerunner of the Royal Ballet) and first performed at Covent Garden on 2 June 1953: the Queen's coronation day. The subject was decided on only at the latest possible moment, and Arnold wrote his forty-minute score in less than a month, and was still adding extra bars to meet the dancers' needs the day before the premiere. *Homage to the Queen* is an allegory; a *divertissement*, in which the queens of the four elements with their trains pay tribute in turn to the newly crowned Elizabeth II. Frederick

Ashton was the choreographer, the ballet being a traditional mix of solos and ensembles, while Arnold's score is also faithful to the traditions of the species. There are gentle waltzes for solo girl dancers, vigorous and emphatically scored variations for solo men, colourful and occasionally grotesque 'characteristic dances', broad and expressive *cantabile* themes in the opening *Prelude* and in the *Pas de deux* at the end of the second and fourth main sections.

The *Prelude*, like the title music of many Arnold film scores, serves to rouse expectation and draw us into the action. Diatonic fanfares (at first distant, quickly loudening) lead into a brisk march *(marziale)* coloured by many passing modulations. This gives way to a broader song-like theme, after which the fanfares return in full force. In the dances that follow Arnold shows how well he understands the functions of the traditional ballet composer and the limits he is expected to observe. The dances are cut in regular eight- and sixteen-bar lengths; there are no contrapuntal complexities, no harmonic shocks or ambiguities, scoring is generally clear-cut and bright, taking account of the fact that the pit orchestra is at psychological and acoustic disadvantage when compared with the concert orchestra. Experienced choreographers and dancers would no doubt be able to supply a genealogy for many of Arnold's dance numbers, in which the music, like the choreography, leans openly on tradition.

Like Tchaikovsky, Arnold is never at a loss for a lively theme that will work out its destiny in thirty-two bars' *presto*, an eight-bar link during which the solo dancer takes up position, or a long-breathed tune that will sustain mood and atmosphere through a full-dress *adagio;* every one of the separate dance sections seems to imply its own specific type of movement. Themes from the *Prelude* return in the short *Epilogue*, and at times a figure from one dance section will reappear in the next. But there is no systematic use of connecting motives – nor, in view of the ballet's mosaic-like structure, is there any dramatic reason why such connections should be made.

As in Britten's *The Prince of the Pagodas*, there is an element of pastiche in tunes, orchestrations, and in the ways in which the musical elements are handled. Perhaps one should 'rather say that both composers pay willing obeisance to admired models. While Britten goes further in evolving a balletic idiom of his own, there are unmistakable Arnold fingerprints in the score of *Homage to the Queen*: in themes, counter-themes, in imaginative orchestration which enlivens the many repetitions of square-cut phrases which the stage demands and, most strikingly, in what might be described as the 'follow-up' sections of the longer, soaring themes, such as the main theme of the extended *pas de deux* in the final *Air*. Arnold's big ballet tunes may at first appear to embrace cliché; but in their continuations, they prove their strength. Many composers might have hit on the opening phrase of the 'big theme' quoted below, with its expectable (G minor^7 – C major^{13}) harmonies; it is the way in which a broad-spanned theme grows and flowers from the first seed that marks the master draughtsman:

Ex.7

Arnold's second ballet, *Rinaldo and Armida* Op. 49, first performed at Covent Garden in January 1955, was again choreographed by Frederick Ashton. A romantic story of the *Giselle–Swan Lake* variety provides the two principals with many opportunities for artful display. Rinaldo, on the way to the Crusades, is lured into Armida's enchanted garden and falls under her spell. Armida knows that she must die if she returns the love of those she has ensnared, but none the less surrenders with a kiss. She dies, and Rinaldo flies in terror as a storm breaks.

Once again, the mood is set in a short introduction, the main theme of which returns at the end of the ballet. Arnold provides Rinaldo and Armida with music more astringent than that of *Homage to the Queen*. Melodies are often chromatic, phrase-lengths no longer measured so strictly in eight-bar lengths. Motives at first associated with the four principal characters (Rinaldo has a companion, Armida a co-enchantress) recur at appropriate moments, the themes of the two main characters are blended as they dance an extended *Pas de deux*.

In *Rinaldo and Armida* Arnold pins his faith on expressive *legato* melody. There are few counter-themes, little decorative or picturesque embellishment. Something of the character of the music is indicated in the extracts below **Ex. 8a** shows the opening motive – expectation-raising, chillingly bleak; **Ex. 8b**, the slow waltz to which Armida first dances; **Ex. 8c**, another Armida theme; which Arnold was later to use as the *Ballad* in his Five Pieces for Violin and Piano (see pp. 133-5)

Ex.8a

Ex.8c

Solitaire was first performed by the Sadler's Wells Theatre Ballet at Sadler's Wells in June 1956. It was described by its choreographer Kenneth MacMillan as 'a kind of game for one', centring round a girl who tries to join in the playground games of her friends, but always ends up on her own. The music comprises the two sets of *English Dances* together with a newly composed *Sarabande* and *Polka*. The serene and long-breathed *Sarabande* provides the centrepiece, another fine *pas de deux*. The *Polka* was designed by Arnold 'to clear the air after the *Sarabande*. Its first bars waken memories of the polka in *Façade*, but it soon turns out to be a piece of quite another character – eccentric, but never facetious, and not in the least inclined to poke fun at other members of the polka family. It is, in fact, a straightforward piece of ballet *grotesquerie*, nearly related to some of the livelier character dances in Tchaikovsky's ballets.

Sweeney Todd Op. 68 was written for the Royal Ballet and first performed by them at Stratford-upon-Avon in December 1959. Space in the Stratford pit was restricted, and Arnold used a reduced orchestra of twelve wind players, timpani, percussion, piano, harp, and strings. The choreographer John Cranko elaborated the story of the demon barber, treating it as comic melodrama or burlesque, inventing many subsidiary characters and a chorus of comic policemen. Production was in toy-theatre style, with a stage revolve in constant use.

This ballet of hectic action was naturally composed on different principles from its predecessors. Arnold provided each of the eight main characters with an identification tag in the form of a short and apt descriptive theme, and throughout shadowed every move or incident in the music (drunken hiccups; proposal of marriage; consternation at discovery of trouser button in meat pie), combining and transforming his motives with much ingenuity. The heroines theme provided material for an extended *Pas de deux* and for a final *Pas de quatre*, both tuneful, expressive, danceable movements; the policemen dance to one of Arnold's livelier comedy themes. But too often and for too long music is forced to play a subservient role and is denied all opportunity for sustained flight.

In his last ballet, Arnold faced the challenge of providing music for one of the greatest and best known of all classical tragedies, and one that offers no scope for diversionary episodes or light relief. *Electra* Op. 79 (first produced at Covent Garden in March 1963, with choreography by Robert Helpmann) covers a little more ground than Strauss's opera, but concentrates the action into a single twenty-five-minute span. The ballet opens with a dance for the Furies, who reappear to crucify Orestes after the murder of Aegisthus. Helpmann piled on the horrors thick, and the music follows suit. The main characters and incidents are vividly portrayed in Arnold's themes: sinuously chromatic for the Furies, lean and muscular for Electra and Orestes, sensuous and spineless for Aegisthus and Clytemnestra:

Ex. 9a (Furies)

Ex. 9b (Electra)

Ex. 9c (Orestes)

Ex. 9d (Aegisthus and Clytemnestra)

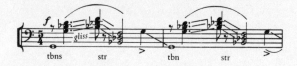

The ballet critic Richard Buckle thought that Arnold's *Electra* music
functioned as film music functions, creating an appropriate
atmosphere without making positive statements on its own account.
It is true that there are few moments when the music seems to *take its
own line* or itself to dictate the action. Choreographers are likely to
approve a score that knows its own place so well; others may wish
that the music more often demanded attention in its own right. The
score of *Electra* is in truth illustrative rather than autonomous, and so
hardly to be judged on the same terms as the major ballet scores of
Stravinsky, Ravel, Bartók, or de Falla. But it has its special place in
Arnold's output, embodying as it does his response to the most
violent, bloody and tragic theme he ever tackled.

6

BREAKING NEW GROUND
Concert Works 1952–61

Skimming through interviews with the more radical young composers of the fifties and sixties, articles on their work, and their own programme notes, we gain an impression of a generation that has determined, like Stravinsky, never to look back; like Boulez, to sweep away the clutter of tradition that slows the rate of advance into new country; like Schoenberg, to hold fast at any cost to the integrity of 'the idea' which is to determine the form, syntax, and instrumentation of each work. If the 'idea' demands that a piece be scored for six bass clarinets, three harps and ocarina, or that a brand-new vocabulary be evolved for its full and true expression, then that is how it must be. The composer, as Virgil Thomson once put it, glories in his integrity and in his role as the unshakeable rock against which the waves of public opinion beat unavailingly.

The traditionalists meanwhile continued to compose for existing instrumental combinations, basing their music in one of the accepted and generally comprehended idioms of the day, referring disparagingly to 'new-music ghettos', affirming their own integrity by steadfastly ignoring the fashions of the moment, digging in their heels all the more firmly because of the pressure of 'accepted opinion' among the younger critics and composers.

This polarization of opinion tended to mask the real issue, which concerns the need to advance rather than the rate of advance. All composers need at various stages in their careers to move on to new ground, to escape from their old selves, as their own characters change and evolve with the passage of time. Those who don't may evolve pleasurable routines of work involving the deployment of subtle skills, but their symphonies, concertos, and operas will ultimately prove dispensable. Traditionalists like Arnold who don't seek to 'make anew' by sweeping away the old order may be dismissed by the radicals as of little account. The crux of the matter, however, lies in the music itself; whether it represents the mixture as before, or whether it marks a genuine advance – in whatever direction – on the composer's journey of self-discovery.

Arnold was himself aware that the Second Symphony marked the end of a particular road; there were to be no more major works in a predominantly lyrical vein, to be enjoyed as 'pure music'. At the same time, he continued to write lighter, entertaining music; the equivalent of Mozartian (or Bartókian) divertimenti. But here too, whether deliberately, or led by instinct or circumstance, he varied the formula for almost every work. Each of the three Sinfoniettas is scored for a different group of instruments; each of the four Concertos written between 1954 and 1960 has its own instrumentation. The oddity of some instrumental ensemble in itself might also act as a spur to inspiration, as in the *Toy Symphony* and the *Grand, Grand Overture* with its vacuum cleaners and floor polisher, both conspicuously successful works. The combined stimulus of a remarkable performer and an unfamiliar or offbeat instrumental set-up was no doubt the best stimulus of all, often providing Arnold with exactly the opportunity *to move on to new ground* that he needed at that particular moment.

Chamber Works

As the orchestral commissions multiplied, Arnold had less time to give to the composition of chamber works; only four were written between 1953 and 1963. The Sonatina for Recorder and Piano Op. 41 is an unassuming piece, demanding no great technical skill, and giving no startling insights into recorder character, but demonstrating the instrument's ability to do simple things beautifully – most of all when it is allowed to stick close to its home tonic: the sixty-six-bar first movement consists of a single span of F major melody with only momentary excursions into foreign keys. The instrument's baroque connections are remembered in the final *Rondo* in which a dotted-note figure from the lively main theme forms the basis for a Handelian central episode in slower tempo. Though the work was published as being suitable for either flute or recorder, from every point of view it is best played on recorder. Music that is carefully composed to stay within the technical range of the recorder while exploiting its particular strengths loses much of its point when played on the instrument which is *capable de tout*. The piano part is designed to support an instrument of low and limited dynamic range; the simplicity of the unmechanized, keyless recorder is reflected in the character of its music.

In the stormy, energetic, highly contrapuntal First Violin Sonata, violin and piano discussed, and often disputed, the main themes at length and almost on equal terms. The more compact and less dramatic Sonata No. 2 for Violin and Piano Op. 43, first performed by Suzanne Rozsa and Paul Hamburger in 1953, is more concerned with thematic transformations than with virtuosity or display. The quietly subversive piano is inclined to question the harmonic implications of the violin's more lyrical themes rather than to initiate ideas of its own. The four short sections are played without a break, and are thematically linked, the opening notes of the violin's first song-like theme appearing in new guise in each movement:

Ex. 1

It is easier to invent an infinitely malleable theme than to devise a scenario in which the drama of growth and change can be convincingly played out; Arnold's transformations are ingenious, but the main theme's character is perhaps not strong enough in the first place for the leading role it is asked to play, while each section is so brief that we seem by the end to have been listening to the précis of a major work rather than the work itself. The scherzo-like second movement (*pizzicato* for the violin for all but a few notes) and the wistful, waltz-like third, in which the main theme, suspended over a static and gently dissonant chordal background, finds no harmonic rest, are none the less strong in atmosphere. The piano's refusal, until the very last bars, to accept the tonal implications of the main theme might well be considered the true subject of the Sonata.

If forced to classify Arnold's Piano Trio Op. 54 of 1956 by style and mood, one might well put it into the same pigeon-hole as Fauré's chamber works with piano. The piano writing is less complex, but the stepwise-moving themes of the first two movements are similarly grave, flowing, and song-like. Though all three movements are tightly organized, the music never advertizes its structural ingenuities, but seems to have flowed from the composer's brain and pen without conscious intellectual effort.

In the opening 3/4 *Allegro con fuoco*, the piano's independent commentary on the strings' first unison theme throws up three distinct motives (**x, y** and **z**), which are to play important roles in later developments:

Ex. 2 (outline only)

In the second movement (4/4 *Andante*) the violin follows the cello in unaccompanied canon; the piano responds with a consoling sequential phrase, and the process repeats in inversion. The emotional temperature rises in a more richly scored central episode, falls again as the canon is resumed. The last movement is a vigorous chaconne (3/4 *Vivace energico*) based on a seven-bar theme that spells out a seven-chord harmonic sequence. The keynote rises a semitone at successive entries moving from D to C sharp at the twelfth, with a final ten bars affirming the return to D. The thematic counterplay is full of incident; Arnold's reductions of the theme to its simplest terms are as intriguing as his elaborations. My only doubt is whether the movement (taken in the context of the whole work) isn't too compact, rushing so quickly to its conclusion that we feel that we have been cheated of the last act of the drama.

The Oboe Quartet Op. 61, written in 1957 to celebrate Leon Goossens's sixtieth birthday, catches the spirit of much eighteenth-century chamber music. Here, as elsewhere in works he has written for great virtuosos, Arnold does not drive his soloist to the very limits of technique. The Quartet is intimate in feeling, seemingly aimed as much at the performers as at the audience, calling for high musicianship rather than for spectacular technical prowess. The opening movement, which celebrates Goossens's elegant phrasing, finesse in decorative passage-work, wide dynamic range and palette of many colours, flows through from first note to last in one broad span, as it establishes a hierarchy of leading and subsidiary themes and motives. The main theme of the slow movement is somewhat in the mood of a famous oboe theme in Tchaikovsky's Fourth Symphony, and shows a similar tendency to backtrack on its course:

Ex.3

Arnold saves one of his finest tunes for late in the movement, while in the final 3/4 *Vivace con brio*, a rondo in the form A–B–A–C–A–B–A, another radiant tune appears in the central episode that alone would have made the movement's fortune. Throughout the Quartet Arnold's melodic inspiration flows as freely as Schubert's, and he squanders memorable themes almost as recklessly. At the same time, he preserves classical balance in the relationship of leading and subsidiary themes and motives, every new tune establishing its right to be heard and staying with us for just the right length of time.

The Quintet for Brass Op. 73, scored for two trumpets, horn, trombone and tuba, was written for the New York Brass Quintet in 1961, at a time when a repertory for this now popular combination hardly existed, and remains one of the most successful entertainment pieces for the ensemble yet produced. Arnold exploited the technical and musical skills of this group of top-class players to the full, writing with particular boldness for trombone and tuba. His intimate knowledge of the medium enabled him to produce strikingly original effects by apparently simple means. No one who has heard the Quintet is likely to forget the weird sound of cup-muted trumpets trailing each other up a whole-tone scale:

Ex.4

The cheerful, athletic outer movements are in the trumpeter's home key of B flat, and make effective use of slurred scale figures and fanfare-like arpeggio figures of the sort that are meat and drink to brass players. Much use is made of canon and close imitation, with occasional excursions into bitonality. In the first movement, trumpets play follow-my-leader games while the three lower instruments unite in graver harmony. In the third, Arnold gets plenty of mileage out of a rising arpeggio that proves to be much more than the introductory cliché formula it first appears to be. The central movement, a chaconne, includes a remarkable episode in which the trombone declaims passionately against sustained harmonies:

Ex.5

Concertos

The first of the three concertos of 1954 was written for Richard Adeney, Arnold's favourite and familiar flautist, for whom the Sonatina of 1948 had also been composed. The flute plays a more spectacular role in the Concerto for Flute and Strings Op. 45 and makes more use of extreme upper registers. No use at all is made of the darkly sensuous lower octave, so lovingly exploited by French composers of the twentieth century. In the lyrical slow movement, the flute never descends below g', in the skittish finale, never below c". Chromaticism is built into many of the main motives as it is not in the Sonatina, but there are various family likenesses between the two works. Both are lyrical, light-hearted, smooth-flowing; conversational rather than argumentative or dramatic in tone. In both first movements, the flute takes the lead in long, almost unbroken melodic paragraphs, and plays the main role in the exposition of thematic material.

Though the orchestra is often involved in the play of imitations, the flute remains throughout the dominant partner, establishing its flighty character at the start in two long paragraphs before settling down to a serene *cantabile* – though, even here, the orchestra's bolero rhythm warns us against taking the soloist too seriously. Most admirable is the way in which Arnold arranges for the flute to maintain a character of innocence and simplicity without ever risking insipidity. Thus, the main theme of the slow movement, which seems at first statement almost bland, is immediately spiced with dissonant appoggiaturas as the violins take over the melody while the flute adds a counter-theme. Family resemblances between first- and second-movement themes assure us that the soloist, in all his moods, retains a single character and identity:

Ex.6

The Concerto for Harmonica and Orchestra Op. 46 was first performed by the dedicatee Larry Adler at a Henry Wood Promenade Concert in August 1954. The solo part is mainly melodic with only a few chordal passages, exposing the instrument in suave *cantabile* themes, in needle-sharp *staccato*, in brilliant runs and glissandos. The orchestra is made up of brass, percussion and strings (which are silent in the central slow movement); any monotony that might arise from the solo instrument's limited dynamic and timbral range is kept at bay by the interest and variety of the often unorthodox instrumentation. The use of tuba or trombone as counter-melodists seems to 'normalize' the agreeably acid tones of the harmonica, which never appears an alien, as it might in a more conventional orchestral context.

The straightforwardly diatonic main theme of the first movement wanders through strange landscapes, an insistent tolling motive providing one of the few stable landmarks:

Ex.7

The slow movement is one of the most striking of Arnold's passacaglias, a sombre little drama based on a seven-bar theme which is repeated five times, a semitone down at each entry, with a short rhythmic episode for percussion and harmonica before the sixth and final statement of the theme. The harmonica takes the first and fourth entries, at other times weaving rhapsodic counterpoints as horns, trombones, trumpets in turn take over the passacaglia theme. The short and lively finale is built round two contrasted tunes; the first with an asymmetric 4 + 4 + 5 bar structure, the second memorably orchestrated, with the harmonica singing in 2/4 high above the strings' C major 6/8:

Ex.8

In the Concerto for Organ and Orchestra Op. 47, written for Denis Vaughan, Arnold uses a Bach-like orchestra of three trumpets (including two piccolo trumpets) timpani and strings, using the

trumpets in consort in eighteenth-century manner to raise the music
to a higher level of brilliance and intensity at key moments. At the
first performance in the Royal Festival Hall in December 1954 Arnold
encouraged Vaughan to make use of the baroque stops of the recently
installed organ. As in much music of the baroque period, interest lies
in draughtsmanship and in the ingenuity with which themes are
manipulated rather than in striking harmonies, textures, timbres, or
even tunes. The gently flowing main theme of the opening 3/4 *Vivace*
seems, by Arnoldian standards, rather tame; but at least it does not
awkwardly reveal the fact that it is born to undergo extraordinary
contrapuntal adventures in the fugal finale. Here, it is transformed
into a 6/8 fugue subject, augmented, treated in close canon, combined
with a grandiose, slow-motion version of itself in the final peroration.
This last movement sustains interest well: Arnold, like Britten, can
turn out a well-sounding orchestral fugue in which textures never
turn to mud, and his contrapuntal resourcefulness is impressive. But
the suspicion remains that he was driven to this display of ingenuity
because the organ itself held little attraction for him.

The Concerto No. 2 for Horn and Strings Op. 58, like the First Horn
Concerto, was composed for Dennis Brain and first performed by him
at the Cheltenham Festival of 1956, only a few weeks before Brain was
killed in a car crash. Though there is much brilliant and taxing music
in the Concerto, Arnold here pays tribute to the musician as much as
to the virtuoso. Many song-like tunes are perfectly adapted to display
Brain's artistry in shaping *cantabile* phrases, the warmth and purity of
his tone, and his clarinet-like fluency. Only the occasional fanfare
passage in the last movement reminds us of the old natural-horn style
or of the instrument's open-air connections. Arnold takes advantage
of Brain's certainty and of his ability to produce beautiful sounds in
stratospheric regions (the soloist once even ascends to f sharp") but
makes less use of lower registers than in the First Concerto; in the first
two movements, the horn very rarely descends below c' (middle c)
and there are no extended passages in the depths.

The first movement (4/4 *Con energico*) is mainly contrapuntal and is
in chamber-music style, the horn very much in the lead, but with the
whole orchestra, including cellos and basses, joining freely in

conversational exchanges. The first rapidly modulating theme establishes no tonal centre; the harmony remains ambiguous even when a more serene second theme arrives. Resolution into the horn's home key of F major is achieved only in the final bars.

The second movement (3/4 *Andantino grazioso*) is mainly lyrical: a languid waltz led by the soloist, with a more vigorous episode based on ascending arpeggio figures, and a harmonically static interlude in which the horn ruminates chromatically against a background of cluster trills before earlier material is recapitulated. The horn's falling phrases in the waltz tune are reminiscent of the *Pas de deux* theme in *Homage to the Queen*, but the emotional atmosphere is cooler.

The several themes of the final 3/4 *Vivace* are well contrasted, and skilfully worked so that cross-connections are unobtrusively established. Once again, it is the horn's clarinet-like fluency rather than military or romantic connections that sets the tone for the movement. The first theme is based on the F major scale with raised fourth and flattened seventh; the second (*legato*) tune opens, like the first, with an upward-leaping octave and hovers on the threshold of F major, which is finally established after a recapitulation of the opening theme and many loud and brilliant pre-cadential fanfares. Arnold's way of teasing and stimulating the listener by *holding off* from F major is original and telling; tension holds until the very last bars. (I am rather sorry that, in Alan Civil's recording, the final emphatic arpeggios with which the horn insists on its own F major-ness have been eliminated.)

In the Harmonica Concerto, with no significant precedents to guide him, Arnold had invented a context in which his soloist could shine and came close to inventing a new character for the solo instrument. A guitar concerto presents a challenge of another sort. The guitar, like the harp, has a familiar but limited range of gestures and special effects and a familiar character-defining repertory. Avant-garde composers who are themselves harpists or guitarists may effectively bend that character, as Carlos Salzédo and Leo Brouwer have demonstrated. Others, in studiously avoiding the clichés and mannerisms that have accrued to the instruments, contrive to leave them devoid of any character at all. Arnold's Concerto for Guitar and

Chamber Orchestra Op. 67, written for and largely inspired by his
friend Julian Bream, and first performed by him in 1959, takes a
bolder course in accepting those clichés and mannerisms as vital and
necessary ingredients without which the portrait would be
incomplete.

Thus, in the outer movements, urbane and brilliant but with a
good line in gentle sentiment, we find conventional *batteries,* rapid
repeated-note figures, harmonic passages conveniently patterned to
lie nicely under the fingers. In these stylish, neo-classical movements,
expressive themes are so lightly accompanied that every nuance in
the shaping of the melodic line can be properly appreciated. The first
movement contains one theme everyone will remember, and that
Bream refers to as 'my meringue': a graceful, easy-going tune that
might well serve as the theme song of a romantic film and that, in the
manner of theme songs, undergoes many literal repetitions (the first
figure, **x**, is also much discusse between soloist and orchestra):

Ex.9

The last movement, like the first, is an urbane and witty piece of
entertainment music, emotionally undemanding, with connections in
the world of neo-classicism. A lively minuet-like theme is developed
in counterpoint and often in canon, later embellished with brilliant
decorations by guitar and woodwind. But the heart of the work lies in
the extended and atmospheric slow movement, which was inspired
by the playing of Django Reinhardt and has an emotional intensity
unequalled in any guitar concerto I know of, and rare enough in any
English music of its period.

The main thematic ingredients are a chromatic figure (**Ex. 10a**); a dramatic skirl for wing (**Ex. 10b**); and a long, open-ended blues theme (not however based on blues harmony) first heard in the guitar's upper register over uneasy rocking harmonies (**Ex. 10a**):

Ex.10a　　　　　　　　　　　Ex.10b

Ex.10c

A 6/8 *vivace* episode perhaps represents a frantic attempt to escape from the mood of sombre resignation that rules in the opening section; but **Ex. 10a** and **b** will not be banished and eventually force a return to the mood and matter of the opening. The movement ends in darkness, muted horn and clarinet reiterating **Ex. 10b** over the guitar's and cellos' tolling Es in lowest registers.

Orchestral Works

Sinfonietta No. 1 Op. 48 was written in 1954 for the Boyd Neel Orchestra, Sinfonietta No. 2 Op. 65 in 1958 for the Jacques Orchestra. They belong to the same family of civilized entertainment pieces as the Serenade for Small Orchestra: lyrical rather than dramatic, lightly scored, clearly structured, close in spirit to the divertimenti of the eighteenth century. No. 1 is scored for oboes, horns and strings, a Mozartian combination that Arnold handles very much in his own manner, horns and oboes sometimes forming a separate and self-contained orchestral chorus, while at other times the first oboe and first horn take on leading melodic roles. The central movement is ingeniously structured, the seven-bar modulating chaconne theme twice giving rise to more restless chromatically inclined episodes between which, with admirable effect, is sandwiched the smoothest and most tranquil version of the main theme, played by three solo violas.

The Second Sinfonietta, scored for flutes, horns and strings, can be thought of as an unassuming younger brother of the Second Symphony; the work as a whole is in its episodes, Haydn-like easy and natural combination of lyrical and contrapuntal. The first movement (3/4 *Allegro non troppo*) opens with a thrice-repeated lyrical theme which is later ironed out to provide an independent and contrasting second subject, and which later lends itself happily to canonic treatment. The wandering, meditative first theme of the slow movement (**Ex. 11a**) is reminiscent of the main theme of the Symphony's slow movement, while the exuberant, dance-inspired finale (**Ex. 11b**) relates closely to the Symphony's finale:

Ex.11a

Ex.11b

The Divertimento No. 2 Op. 24 was composed for the National Youth Orchestra, and first performed by them in 1950. Ten years later, Arnold revised the work, replacing the second movement (originally a *Tango*) with a *Nocturne*. This new version, Op. 75, was first performed in Liverpool in October 1961 by the Royal Liverpool Philharmonic Orchestra, Lawrence Leonard conducting.

The Divertimento is in three movements, playing for only nine minutes in all. The first movement (*Fanfare*, 4/4 *Allegro*) combines bold brass fanfares with brilliant third-based semiquaver passages for strings and woodwind, with just one short and striking phrase for woodwind that can be labelled as a motive in its own right. The central *Nocturne* (4/4 *Lento*) punctuates successive entries of an expressive five-bar theme (later extended) with a series of sighs – falling seconds that move from dissonance to consonance in the traditional manner.

The last, and most substantial movement is a *Chaconne* (3/4 *Allegro con spirito*) based on a non-modulating eight-bar harmonic sequence, repeated thirteen times. After a loud and vigorous statement followed by two double variations, variations 6 and 7 (which are nearly-related to one another) form a tranquil interlude before the final build-up to a full-orchestra recapituation of the theme in its original form. There is no exploration of unfamiliar territory in the Divertimento; but the work forms an effective short display piece for the orchestra, and particularly for trumpets and trombones.

The trombone passage in the Brass Quintet gave us a hint that under the skin of the urbane and tuneful composer of sonatinas, sinfoniettas, and elegant chamber music there was a wilder man waiting to get out and lay about him. But such declamatory, almost rhapsodic passages are not common in Arnold's concert works. In the overture *Tam O'Shanter* Op. 51, however, Arnold seized the chance to write illustrative music in which inhibitions could legitimately be cast aside, as the headlong ride of the hero is illustrated in boisterous, disruptive music. The Scottish flavour is of course strong: in the elaborate decorative passages for paired bassoons and for solo trombone in the introduction recalling the music of the pibrochs, in the use of Scottish snaps and primitive drone harmonies, shifting in whole tones. But while plenty of composers have seized on these obvious characteristics of Scottish music to parody or imitate, few have so imaginatively and boldly translated bagpipe music into orchestral terms.

Compared with *Beckus*, *Tam O'Shanter* is rowdy, frantic, unrestrained, and for that reason less likely to appeal to highbrow music-lovers. But there is much originality in the orchestration, and impetus never flags. As in *Beckus*, there are echoes of *Till Eulenspiegel*, particularly in the little inserts that briefly refer to past episodes in Tam's lurid career (tiny fragments of dance music for two piccolos, and the three bars of solemn church music that precede the final *Presto*). Like Strauss, Arnold will at one moment drive home the message insistently with extravagant use of the whole orchestral apparatus, at the next will be content with a hint, delivered in the most concise and economical terms.

The *Four Scottish Dances* Op. 59, completed in 1957, were first performed by the BBC Concert Orchestra (conducted by the composer) later that year. If their Scottishness is more evident than the Englishness of the two earlier sets of dances, that is readily explainable when one considers that Scottish folk music has a more strongly marked national character than the English variety, and that the second dance is in fact based on one of Robert Burns's songs. (This movement had its origins in the film score for *The Beautiful County of Ayr*, in which the bassoon's augmentation of the main theme in the *meno mosso* section accompanied the appearance of a prize bull in the auctioneer's ring.)

The scoring is less bizarre than that of *Tam O'Shanter*, the uncomplicated open-air flavour of the music far removed from the fevered fantasy of the comedy overture. Scotticisms in the form of imitations of bagpipers or folk fiddlers are avoided. But Arnold finds stimulus in the angular tunes and stamping rhythms of Scottish folk music. Nos. 1, 2, and 4 are of primitive vigour, suitable for the use of merrymakers in a cold climate. The serene and delicately orchestrated third dance (*Allegretto*) clearly comes from the same stable as the seventh *English Dance*, even though the rhythmic snaps built into the tune establish a Scottish connection:

Ex. 12a   Scottish Dances, No. 3

Ex. 12b   English Dances, No. 7

7

MUSIC FOR VOICES

All his adult life Arnold has written for instruments with an insider's understanding, and remained in close touch with many of the leading instrumentalists of the day. His practical contacts with singers have been fewer, and he has not often been inspired by the virtuosity or artistry of particular performers in this area. He tends to write for voices rather as he writes for the piano: with scrupulous regard for the limitations of the medium and of averagely equipped performers, seemingly motivated by no particular desire to exploit the human voice in new or surprising ways.

His passion for direct and clear statement and his respect for the written word partly account for his favouring word-to-a-note settings, without wide leaps, elaborate melismata or decorative passages. He shows little interest in the more sensuous or personal qualities of the solo voice; in almost every instance, the clear delivery of the verbal message takes priority over all other considerations. There are songs and part-songs among Arnold's earliest works, and he has continued throughout his career to compose for voices; but the total number of vocal works is small. With few exceptions they lie well off the main track of Arnold's development and give little evidence of the evolution of a distinctive Arnold vocal idiom. Anyone who was handed the undated scores of the *John Clare Cantata* of 1955, the *Five William Blake Songs* of 1959, and the *Two John Donne Songs* of 1973 would be hard put to it to arrange them in chronological order.

Operas and Cantatas

In the bulk of the vocal works involving instruments as well as voices much of the character and melodic interest lies in the instrumental commentary. In both operas and in all four cantatas, the usual division of labour is between voices as message-bearers, orchestra as commentator. The balance is thus nearer to being Wagnerian than Verdian – yet quite un-Wagnerian in that instruments at all times wait assiduously on the voices, never monopolizing, rarely even competing for attention.

Twenty-five pages in full score is all that was ever written of *Henri Christophe*. The opera, set in Haiti in 1811, was planned in response to the Arts Council's scheme for commissioning operas for the Festival of Britain in 1951, but abandoned when the outline plan was rejected by the panel of judges. Already a pattern emerges: atmospheric orchestration sets the scene, while words are set in near-naturalistic recitative, often in conjunct motion, with little overlapping of voices in ensemble to obscure the sense.

Joe Mendoza, who provided the libretto for *Henri Christophe*, also wrote the libretto of Arnold's next opera, *The Dancing Master* Op. 34, a one-act comedy of intrigues and misunderstandings adapted from William Wycherley's *The Gentleman Dancing Master*. A virtuous heroine (Miranda) is wooed by a foppish Frenchman and by the more manly Gerard, who makes her acquaintance by climbing in through her window; there is a maid eager to be a party to any intrigues or seductions that are in the offing; a watchful aunt-duenna determined to save Miranda's reputation from real and imagined dangers; a hot-headed Spanish father whose unexpected appearance further complicates the plot.

Gerard pretends to be a dancing master, which opens the way for a number of formal dances which (as in Mozart or Verdi) provide a background for dialogue. Spanish rhythms and orchestration colour the music of Miranda's father; the Frenchman woos Miranda to a lute song, while a sustained ensemble of perplexity for five characters is superimposed on a slow galliard. As in the play, emotions are formalized, the characters never stepping out of the frame, while Arnold's urbane and melodious score warns us against taking their problems and passions too seriously. *The Dancing Master* has something in common with eighteenth-century ballad opera, even more with the lighter operas of Wolf-Ferrari based on Goldoni, which it resembles in flirting with pastiche, in transparent orchestration, with the orchestra often setting the mood and the pace, in the use of diatonic harmony lightly spiced with dissonance, and more generally in the ways in which high sophistication hides behind a mask of mock-simplicity.

If the soufflé fails to rise, the librettist must take a good share of the blame. Many scenes are too wordy for the good of the music, episodes are too loosely linked together, and as a result the action tends to move by fits and starts or to hang fire. It takes a more skilful and experienced craftsman than Mendoza to distil a good libretto from the witty repartees and games of bluff and double-bluff of seventeenth-century comedy.

For Sidney Gilliat, librettist of Arnold's next opera, *The Open Window,* the problem was not how to condense but how to expand, so as to give the characters of a three-page Saki story substance and credibility enough to sustain them through a forty-minute opera. Gilliat proved equal to the occasion, and provided Arnold with the best libretto he was ever to set.

The main characters are Franton Nuttel, a hypochondriac who comes to the country in search of total peace, and the fifteen-year-old Vera, a girl whose speciality is 'romance at short notice'. Vera persuades Nuttel that her absent uncles lost their lives in a tragic accident three years before ('Poor aunt is always convinced that they will come back some day and walk in through the window just as they used to do.'). When the flesh-and-blood uncles with their dog are seen approaching in the twilight (singing, as Vera prophesied, 'Bertie, why do you bound?'), Nuttel loses his nerve and bolts, leaving Vera to make up another lurid story to explain his action to her puzzled family (he had once been hunted into a newly dug grave near the Ganges by a pack of pariah dogs, and naturally has a horror of all dogs . . .).

Arnold's music moves at brisk conversational pace, sparely and surely establishing character and mood. An innocent-seeming melodic motive suggests the peace and quiet of the country retreat, but is subject to jumpy transformations as Nuttel's jangled nerves get the better of him. He eagerly pours out his medical history to the sympathetic Vera against a background of semitonal dissonances and twisted chromaticisms; Vera responds with a dramatic monologue supported by an uneasily shifting two-bar ground (the same motive returns when she begins to spin her latest fantasy at the end of the opera):

Ex. 1

Gilliat's main addition to the story lies in the expansion of Nuttel's medical history (only alluded to in the story) into a saga of consultations and radiological tests ('My Babinski test was normal and there wasn't any lesion . . .') set as a sort of patter song – there is no stopping Nuttel once he has started on the description of his symptoms. The returning uncles sing 'O, it's my delight on a shiny night' rather than the now forgotten 'I say, Bertie . . .' and the story Vera invents to explain Nuttel's sudden exit is altered. In other respects, Gilliat sticks closely to the original. Arnold, in a score even sparer than that of *The Dancing Master,* is meticulous as ever in not allowing music to obscure word. *The Open Window,* which is scored for chamber orchestra and lasts about twenty-two minutes, would make an excellent curtain-raiser for any small company, professional, student, or amateur, that could call on the right sort of singing actor and actress to play Nuttel and Vera.

A more substantial and ambitious stage work, the Nativity masque

Song of Simeon Op. 69, followed less than two years later. This was written for a charity matinée in aid of refugee children held at Drury Lane Theatre in January 1960. The masque opens with an Annunciation scene, after which the action moves from stable to inn. Here we meet Simeon, summoned to Bethlehem to pay his taxes, and the children Susana and Arak with their mother. Christopher Hassall's highly professional libretto provides cues for song, dance and some painfully humorous interludes. The churlish innkeeper refuses the newcomers admission in a glib patter song; the four shepherds also turn out to be comedy characters; Susana wins a night's lodging for her family by dancing (Arnold provides a picturesque and effective mock-oriental number). Night falls, and it is left to Arak, gazing out into the auditorium, to describe the scene in the manger: 'I can see a woman running with a bowl, and those four shepherds who were here just now . . . they've hung an enormous lantern over the door . . .'. The whole cast join in singing the hymn 'On Jordan's Bank' and Simeon ends the masque with a short and straightforward setting of the Nunc Dimittis.

It can never be easy to turn out yet another Nativity masque, and Hassall's workmanlike libretto at least provides plenty of opportunities for a resourceful composer. But the stilted librettist's English and the feeling that the ground has been transversed many times diminish the work's impact. Once again music serves word and theme faithfully. (Rather too faithfully? Consider by contrast how, in *L'Enfance du Christ*, Berlioz's own words provide no more than the starting point for strange flights of fancy and imagination.) The Annunciation music and the Nunc Dimittis are written in a euphonious ecclesiastical style and are apt enough in the context. There are catchy tunes for the people at the inn and the shepherds; the linking narrative passages are skilfully integrated into the whole, action and music flowing smoothly throughout the hour-long masque. Yet the most striking music of all is to be found in the passage for instruments only that precedes and follows the Annunciation scene. Reiterated rising seconds on the brass are answered by a tolling theme on tuned percussion; a memorable double-motive of archaic simplicity creates just the right mood of solemn expectation:

Ex.2

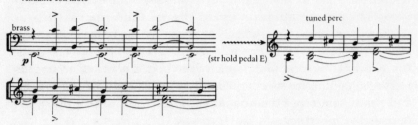

The cantata *The Return of Odysseus* Op. 119 was written for the combined choirs of the Schools' Music Association and first performed at the Royal Albert Hall in 1977. With young amateur performers in mind, the poet Patric Dickinson recast the story in simple colloquial English and without indulging in a single poetic metaphor. He preludes the story of the return with an extended account of Odysseus' more hair-raising early adventures. Penelope's woes and the destruction of the suitors are described almost dispassionately, as it might be by child witnesses who were not themselves involved in the action. Arnold in turn treats the text simply and directly. Narrative passages are set word-to-a-note and mostly in melodious, metrical arioso. There are memorable tunes; voice parts are considerately laid out, avoiding awkward jumps and hard-to-pitch intervals. While the voices are often used tellingly, it is the orchestra that builds up tension through the use of repeated and insistent rhythmic figures, dramatic dissonance, repeated ostinato figures.

The music of *Odysseus*, appropriate to the text and to the original occasion, is also apt for performance by amateur adult choirs of modest pretensions. Yet neither *Simeon* nor *Odysseus* are among Arnold's more personal works. In both he seems to follow the lead given him by his librettist so closely that his own character is subordinated in the process. It is as if he carried over into these works the attitudes of the film composer, whose business it is to enhance dramatic effects rather than to strike out a line of his own.

There is, however, one cantata in which Arnold, without distortion or elaboration, not only transcends his texts but creates from a heterogeneous anthology of poems a unified and wholly characteristic work, stronger and more urgent in its emotional appeal than any of the earlier choral pieces. *Song of Freedom* Op. 109 was written for the twenty-first anniversary of the National Schools Brass Band Association in 1973, and was designed to be performable by an average school band and choir. Arnold himself chose the words from poems on freedom written by children and entered for a competition sponsored by the NSBBA. Often naive, sometimes falling into cliché, the poems have a sort of innocent passion and sincerity that is mirrored in the music.

In the *Prelude*, subdued fanfares herald a Whitmanesque 'freedom song' ('From the four corners of the globe, the muted introduction to the "Freedom Song" is heard . . .'). This unison stanza song in 3/4 is punctuated by interludes (for voices and band) which take up the themes of the introduction, while a central 6/8 section introduces new material. An optimistic *Hymn* set in the style of Moody and Sankey and without a suspicion of parody or sophistication follows ('Earth will be one country, every man our friend . . .'). A three-part *Intermezzo* (dirge, syncopated central *allegro* and blues) contrasts the wretchedness of famine victims and of the old and handicapped with the selfish pleasure-seeking of the prosperous Westerner ('I'm fine, I've got food, so why would I care? Half the world is starving; I know it's unfair . . .'). The work ends with an exultant C major hymn to freedom, plainly harmonized and set over a marching bass.

In the other choral works, we are often aware of the adaptable craftsman applying his skills to a particular task, conscientiously, but without strong personal involvement. In *Song of Freedom*, Arnold identifies fully with his child librettists. Music, forms, idioms, textures and harmonies spring direct from the words. I doubt whether Arnold was directly influenced by Weill, but there are striking stylistic parallels with Weill's middle-period works: in the unapologetic use of popular idioms; in the bleak harmony of introduction and dirge; in the sombre wind-band scoring; in the plainness of word-setting which suggests that, in dealing with grim and urgent topics, the one thing that matters is to get the message over clearly; in the abrupt alternations between sombre, almost hieratic moods and moods of feverish gaiety; even in certain turns of phrase:

Ex.3

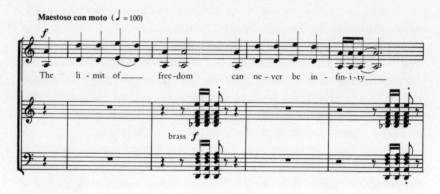

The li - mit of___ free - dom can ne - ver be in - fin - i - ty___

brass *f*

Arnold's popular, 'commonplace' music, like Weill's, is not genre music, the product of a superior composer masquerading as the poor man's Verdi (or Bernstein; or Moody and Sankey); it's the real thing. In both cases, the certainty of musical draughtsmanship and the effectiveness of unorthodox formal procedures reveal the hand of the fully equipped and resourceful composer. But Arnold, like Weill, makes no attempt to conciliate the highbrows with in-jokes or technical refinements that would declare, 'In spite of all, I am really one of you!'.

Shorter Choral Works and Song-Cycles

I doubt if many would recognize Arnold's hand in *Psalm 150: Laudate Dominum* Op. 25, a setting of the Psalm for choir and organ written for the choir of St Matthew's, Northampton, in 1950; in the (unaccompanied) Two Ceremonial Psalms for Treble Voices written for the wedding of Anne Mendoza in 1952, or in the *Song of Praise* Op. 55 for unison voices and piano (words by John Clare) commissioned for the jubilee of Wycombe Abbey School in 1956. There could never be any doubt, however, that they belong to an English tradition, or more specifically to the Anglican tradition of soundly made, deliberately anonymous, Church music. All nevertheless must have been appropriate to the various occasions, while the organ interludes in *Laudate Dominum* are ingenious and effective.

Arnold returned to his favourite Northampton poet in the *John Clare Cantata* Op. 52 for SATB chorus and piano duet, commissioned by William Glock for the Dartington Summer School of 1955. The six poems follow the seasons from winter round to winter. No doubt with the Summer School context in mind, Arnold provided a work harmonically more sophisticated than the earlier choral pieces, calling for a choir that would be able to attack and sustain unfamiliar and dissonant chords with confidence.

Clare's poems are set plainly but lyrically. The pianists provide appropriately patterned backgrounds based on independent figurations on the Schubert – Britten pattern. The first song ('Winter is come in earnest') is a flowing 9/8, lyrical but rueful; the pianists' triplets flavour the music with gentle but persistently clashing sevenths. The second ('The insect world now sunbeams higher climb') is a brittle march with an illustrative piano part based on crushed harmonies and melodic figures, reminiscent of Britten's accompaniment to Blake's 'Little fly, thy summer's play . . .' (but Arnold's setting pre-dates Britten's by several years):

Ex. 4

John Clare Cantata
The Insect World

Britten: Blake Songs
The Fly

The third is a spring pastoral with drone bass; the fourth accompanies a description of summer insects ('Tiny loiterers on the barley beard') with a bees' wedding (or spinning-wheel) accompaniment. The unaccompanied fifth ('The spring is gone, the summer beauty wanes . . .') is a mainly homophonic part-song with some poignant discords, which looks back in sorrow. A short epilogue frames the cycle by reverting to the music and words of the first song.

The *Five William Blake Songs* Op. 66 for alto and strings were written for Pamela Bowden, and first performed by her with the Richmond Community Centre String Orchestra in March 1959, Arnold conducting. This is another of the very few works that makes one think of Britten. The first song, 'O holy virgin! Clad in purest white', has something of the radiance of the *Nocturne*, 'Blow bugle blow!', in the *Serenade* Op. 31 for tenor, horn and strings; the orchestral rhetoric is also of the same type:

Ex.5

The setting of 'My silks and fine array' (No. 4) as a sombre, narrow-intervalled funeral march is also Brittenish, though the textures of Arnold's songs are generally less elaborate, the harmonies simpler, the accompaniment patterns more regular, than in the Britten cycles. Writing for an admired singer, he treats the solo voice with sympathy but does not, like Britten, glory in vocal extravaganzas or in the voice itself as the supreme musical instrument. Yet interest is varied and well sustained, and at many points the music matches the bright innocence of Blake's words.

Arnold has more than once said that good poetry needs no crutch, and shouldn't be set to music. He did, nevertheless, in 1974 set 'The Good-Morrow' and 'Woman's Constancy' in *Two John Donne Songs* Op. 114(b). The writing for voice is mostly sober and unsensual; piano accompaniments are plain and wait on the voice; there are no harmonic surprises. It is as though he was too much inhibited by his respect for the words to attempt any miracles of transformation.

8

SHOCKS AND SURPRISES
Third, Fourth and Fifth Symphonies

Admirers of the lyrical, life-affirming Second Symphony would no doubt have welcomed a third, fourth and fifth symphony of like nature. But the serene and optimistic mood of the earlier works could hardly be maintained by a composer living in the real world in the mid-twentieth century. Arnold seems to have been conscious that the time for untroubled singing was past. In the three symphonies that followed, he was to extend the technical and emotional range of his music, to question the conventional concept of 'symphony' by including popular elements, and to allow a more personal, idiosyncratic and unsettling note to be heard.

Nevertheless, Symphony No. 3 Op. 63 (first performed by the Royal Liverpool Philharmonic Orchestra in December 1957) resembles the Second in many respects. The new work is again based on lyrical or dance-like themes; there is once more a cheerful, light-hearted, Haydnish finale. Textures are generally spare and transparent, with few massive or bludgeoning *tuttis* and many passages of chamber-music intimacy. The overall tone of voice is again discursive rather than argumentative – there is no interaction between the two main themes of the first movement.

The prevailing mood of the Third Symphony is, however, very different from that of the Second. In place of calm assurance, we encounter a troubled, questioning lyricism. Arnold himself has remarked that the basic plot of the work resembles that of Sibelius's Fifth Symphony. The course of dramatic developments, however, is a good deal less clear-cut. One critic complained, after the first performance, that the symphony consisted largely of orchestral 'effects'. There is perhaps a danger that the originality of instrumentation may distract the listener from the thematic plot. This is one of many occasions when to appreciate Arnold's music one needs not only a mind free of preconceptions but a new balance of attention.

In the first bars, harmony touches on E major, B flat major, E flat major, and E major again before **Ex. 1** appears in full (on cellos and violas, then first violins):

Ex. 1

The hesitant opening bars prove in due course to have been rather more than a preparatory clearing of the throat before the real business begins. They foreshadow the uncertain harmonic course of the questing main theme, and recur twice during the movement, suggesting that doubts have not been resolved.

Though the falling bass line of **Ex. 1** suggests order and stability, even offers a sort of tonal anchorage, the tonality of the theme itself is indeterminable. But a second theme, which appears many times with clear major harmony, brings harmonic stability:

Ex. 2

(continued)

Apart from the use of the attendant-fourth motive, **y**, in central developments, this theme is never fragmented or mined for subsidiary motives. The main subject of discussion and transformation is the head motive **x** from **Ex. 1**, while agitated passages in *staccato* thirds also play an important role.

There is no question here of the 'contrived drama' of many post-Beethoven sonata movements. Though there is some development of **x**, the character and atmosphere of the movement derive as much from changes of orchestral scenery as from thematic transformations. **Ex. 1** does, in time, reappear in its original non-key and is repeated, as before, a fourth higher, but the return is contrived so quietly and undramatically that it has little of the effect of a formal recapitulation.

Soon, tension rises as the fourth-motive, **y**, comes to the fore, and the tempo changes to 6/8 *Vivace*. One more reference to the opening bars, and a vigorous new figure in sevenths (**Ex. 3a**) appears, while a new theme (**Ex. 3b**), derived from **Ex. 1**, plays a subsidiary role:

Ex.3a

Ex.3b

Ex. 1 returns, rhythmically transformed and reharmonized. The never dense textures thin still further as **Ex. 2** makes a final appearance on flute and the movement ends with fleeting reference to **x** and **y**.

The second movement (4/4 *Lento*) opens with a solemnly expressive eight-bar melody for unison strings, twice repeated with an added counter-theme. At the third repetition (shown in **Ex. 4**), the underlying harmonies are spelt out, and we begin to suspect that Arnold intends a passacaglia.

Ex. 4

Instrumentation and patterning tend to follow the eight-bar structure
of the passacaglia; but because the main theme steals in and catches
us unawares, because of the slow tempo (each variation takes about
two minutes) and because the harmonic sequence is too disjointed to
be easily perceived as a harmonic unit, we are little aware of the
movement's sectional structure. There are, in fact, twenty consecutive
repetitions of the harmonic sequence, occasionally extended to nine
or ten bars. The original melody, which after the opening threefold
statement is heard only once more in its complete form (in the
fifteenth variation) provides most of the material for development.
The semiquaver figure in the second and eighth bars, **x**, appears in
many contexts and could be accounted the thematic hero of the
movement; another motive derived from **y** also plays a leading role:

Ex.5

Sections 5-6 and 12-13 are double variations of identical character,
in which quiet imitative figures form a blurred and static background
to longer melodic phrases based on **y**, provide contrast and serve as
rest areas. The movement ends with two *fortissimo* variations in which
x is repeatedly delivered at maximum intensity.

Arnold does not attempt to resolve the harmonic ambiguities and
tensions of the passacaglia. Instead, taking the course often followed
by Haydn after one of his strangely modulating slow movements, he
serves up a vigorous, cheerful, entirely straightforward finale.

Ex.6a

Ex.6b

The tail of **Ex. 6a** twists in various directions at various times, but there is no mystery about the connection between **Exx. 6a** and **b**. A third theme, less skittish but more purposefully energetic, provides necessary ballast:

Ex.7

Arnold plays resourcefully with this material, thematic and instrumental invention going hand in hand. Just as we think the finishing line is in sight, the movement takes a fresh lease of life with the appearance of a new tune (twice repeated) in which one can still trace the rising and falling thirds of **Ex. 7**:

Ex.8

str 𝆑 cantabile .... 𝆑𝆑

Fuguing and augmentation based on **z** then lead rapidly to a loud and imposing conclusion in which Arnold seems to be sending up his light-hearted tunes by pretending, for a brief moment, to take them entirely seriously.

Symphony No. 4 op. 71 was commissioned by the BBC, and first performed at the Royal Festival Hall in London by the BBC Symphony Orchestra in November 1960, Arnold himself conducting. Though this performance took place in the concert hall, Arnold was surely aware that he was addressing a far larger audience of radio listeners with little experience of 'serious' concert music, and seized the opportunity to include explicitly popular elements in the new work. The Symphony, composed in the aftermath of the Notting Hill race riots, makes use of instruments and rhythms associated with West Indian popular music. A gesture of solidarity was thus written into the Symphony; though one can be reasonably sure that the gesture would not have taken this form if the musician in Arnold had not been fascinated by Caribbean music.

The orchestra is a large one, including piccolo, contrabassoon, celesta, harp, with bongos, marimbaphone, and tom-toms – all, at that time, rare visitors to the concert hall – added to the usual percussion. The first two join immediately in the foreplay of the opening *Allegro*: eleven bars of descending-scale passages in or about A minor, shared between woodwind, harp and marimba, with sharp interjections from bongos. Percussion then retreat from the scene during the twofold statement of the first theme, a gentle 'white-note' tune in the Lydian mode, lightly and luminously scored:

Ex.9

A more robust passage for full brass and percussion based on a rising-third motive declares for G major; the material so far introduced is further discussed and elaborated before a new motive appears against a percussive ostinato involving both timpani and exotic instruments:

Ex. 10

There has been nothing so far in themes or treatments that could cause the purist to raise an eyebrow; the 'exotic' instruments have been, so to speak, adopted into the family on equal terms, and have mixed in with the established percussion without causing disruption. The scene seems to be set for an eventful and dramatic development section in which the well-contrasted themes so far introduced will work out their destinies. But at this point, Arnold pulls the chair away from beneath us. Over a syncopated, *staccato* accompaniment of the plainest I–II–V–I character in B flat (home key of so much popular music) unison violins and violas (muted) offer us a song-like theme that seems to have strayed into the Symphony from another world, harmonized and scored in a manner that will be familiar to all devotees of commercial entertainment music of a certain vintage; a tune seemingly designed, with its many reiterations of the opening figure, to work its way into the listener's memory and to stay there:

Ex. 11

Ex. 11 at once repeats in canon with itself, with added smears on woodwind which further stress the pop-music connection. By this

time, x has already been heard eighteen times. This completes the exposition. Earlier themes are next developed and extended, with the head phrase of Theme 1 coming in for imitative treatment. Caribbean instruments again intervene even more fiercely than before as sharply accented syncopated chords are projected against a wall of percussive sound. The tumult subsides, and we return home to a reworking of **Ex. 10** with the scale figures of the opening integrated into the music. In the free recapitulation, the pop theme is heard twice more – the first time, luminously scored, celesta and harp taking the tune in canon against the strings' syncopated *pizzicato*. **Ex. 10** is also heard against the same background – suggesting, maybe, the possibility of reconciliation? A possibility strengthened when the movement ends with the final return of **Ex. 11** in F major, followed by reminiscences of **Ex. 10**, also in its original Lydian F.

Caribbean instruments play only subsidiary roles in the slippery, eel-like scherzo, based on very short motives and full of *sotto voce* grotesqueries (Berlioz's Queen Mab and Holst's Mercury are surely among this movement's ancestors). One canonic passage must be quoted, as illustrating Arnold's ability to create original and memorable effects with the simplest means:

Ex.12

The rapidity with which ideas succeed one another is both exhilarating and disorientating. But a more sober trio, neo-baroque in character, gives us time to regain our breath. An eight-bar clarinet tune, punctuated by *pizzicato* chords, is repeated in turn by oboe, bassoon, and trumpet, in ascending sequence of minor keys (A, C sharp, F, A); the answering eight-bar phrase, which is repeated three and a half times, in the same key sequence, turns out to be a retrograde inversion of the first phrase.

Ex.13

When the scherzo returns, this too retraces its steps in almost literal retrograde, back to the first bar. This apparently intellectual mode of composition is validated by the fact that we don't guess what is in store for us until well past the halfway mark. Critics at the first performance do not seem to have spotted the retrogrades either – or if they did, chose not to mention them.

The languorous 3/4 *Andantino* opens with a three-minute paragraph of unbroken *legato* melody, the main elements in which are shown below:

Ex.14a

Ex.14b

Ex.14c

'Development' is a side-issue in a movement that draws its character from its themes' inviolability. **Ex. 14b** operates always within the narrowest range as though unable to escape from its own obsessions; the more expansive **Ex. 14c** brings relief. At times, the music takes on the character of a slow, dreamy waltz; luminous instrumentation gives the music an almost voluptuous flavour. Arnold is as well aware as any composer of the dangers of schmaltz or cliché. He is also courageous enough to admit them into his music when the context demands it. Here, unusually, he allows the cellos to sing freely in tenor register, the horn to add its expectable and sententious comment to **Ex. 14c**.

Once again, as in the Third Symphony, the mood changes abruptly as the last movement opens (*Con fuoco*) with a lively and vigorous theme; in this case, a fugue subject that might be labelled schoolmasterly if each entry were not rudely and regularly interrupted in mid-course by a ferocious chromatic figure(*ff possibile*):

Ex.15

Imitative counter-themes accumulate round the fugue theme as it is
stated eight times alternately in tonic and dominant (F major and C
major). The whole orchestra soon becomes involved in the action. A
contrasting *espressivo legato* theme in or round about D minor
(woodwind, then upper strings in unison) follows:

Ex. 16

Syncopated woodwind chords over ostinato bass prepare the way for
the return of **Ex. 15** and **Ex. 16**, both in their original keys. The
Caribbean instruments, so far silent, now enter with their own version
of the fugue subject – even though contrapuntal detail is swallowed up
in the cheerful din, its rhythmic contours are by now familiar enough
for us to realize what they are about. Black and white musics are now
working to the same ends, with the syncopated motive returning in
imposing crescendo as though working up to a grandiose peroration.

But Arnold has one more shock in store for us: at this moment, the full orchestra breaks without warning into a brutal *Alla marcia*, led from below by all bass instruments in unison, with ferocious military skirls in extreme upper registers from the upper woodwind:

Ex. 17

This warlike interlude, thematically unrelated to all that has gone before, is cut into the movement in cinematic fashion. Forty-seven bars on, we revert, equally abruptly, to 3/4 and to the fugue subject, at last heard in continuous form above an ostinato derived from the brass interjection x. A *Maestoso* version of the same theme follows, and the movement ends, in apparent triumph, with horns reiterating the opening figure of the fugue subject in Lydian F major.

For those who seek to interpret the message behind the notes, the Fourth Symphony poses two enigmas. What is the significance of the so-easy-to-digest pop tune of the first movement, which is never developed or referred to in the rest of the Symphony, but which fixes itself insistently in the memory? Why does that rude and warlike march break into the finale like an alien from another world of music?

The pop tune, belonging neither to concert hall nor to Caribbean worlds, could be taken to represent the bland voice of commercial music, which pursues its course indifferent both to social problems and to the latest developments in the world of 'serious music'. The trouble with that view is that the pop tune (like the march tune) is no mere symbol. It leads its own musical life; whether we like it or hate it, it compels attention and some sort of emotional involvement.

I am not sure, though, whether Arnold had foreseen the full consequences of this bold piece of musical cookery. In popular songs built on the invariable verse-plus-refrain pattern, it is the refrain that counts for all; often it seems as though composers labour to make the verse unmemorable so as to divert attention to the refrain. In a symphony, a different balance obtains; a tune that makes no concessions to its surroundings and that is so memorable that it tends to usurp all our attention can't be so easily accommodated.

It is tempting, and fairly plausible, to 'explain' the march episode in the finale as representing the senseless intervention of military might, which puts an end to civilized activities but which, in the aftermath, leaves matters precisely as they were, nothing achieved, nothing solved. But music doesn't explain itself so easily. There is something exhilarating in the vigour and crudity of the interpolated music that wins us over to its side. Like Weill's and Shostakovich's brutal marches, which manage simultaneously to horrify and to appeal to the Nazi or Stalinist in all of us, it tells us things about ourselves we would prefer not to know. But Arnold (like Weill and unlike Shostakovich) gives nothing away, nor is there a hint of parody in his 'popular' or military motives. The musical contrast between ingenious fuguing and robust homophonic *Alla marcia* is undoubtedly striking and 'effective' – could that be all there is to it? The question is unanswerable – no amount of speculation or analysis can resolve such paradoxes or penetrate the hidden truths that are locked into the music itself.

Symphony No. 5 Op. 74 was commissioned by the Cheltenham Festival Society and first performed at Cheltenham in July 1961 by the Hallé Orchestra, the composer conducting. The musical action of the first movement conforms to no clearly structured plan; the tone of voice, as in the Third Symphony, is generally discursive. But a brief look at the score reveals that in certain respects this is one of the most strictly organized movements Arnold has ever written.

It opens without preamble with a five-note motive on oboe, **Ex. 18a**, twice repeated, answered by *pizzicato* chords, **Ex. 18b**. Harp and celesta then woodwind, take over the chord sequence; a chromatic motive and its inversion appear *fortissimo* in the bass, **Ex. 18c**.

Ex. 18a

Ex. 18b

Ex. 18c

By this time, less than thirty seconds into the movement, it will perhaps have dawned on the listener that some unfamiliar organizing force is at work. The odd harmonies of the chord sequence **Ex. 18b** are in fact created by running a series of two-note chords in harness with their own retrogrades. The sequential, diatonic theme that follows seems, however, to come from another more stable and familiar world of music. This first appears on tuned percussion, detail blurred as though we were viewing the music through gauze or thin mist:

Ex.19

When yet another *legato* theme appears on cellos, it turns out to be closely related both to **Ex. 18a** and to **Ex. 18b**:

Ex.20

This is a type of melody we have not hitherto come across in Arnold's music: lyrical in character, but eschewing formal symmetries and question-and-answer-type phrasing, having more in common with Wagner's 'endless melodies' than with the classical or neo-classical themes that have so often provided the models for Arnold's shapely tunes.

Throughout the movement, there is limited interplay between chromatic and diatonic elements, and it is the chromatic motives that provide most of the material for debate and transformation. **Ex. 18b** and **Ex. 18c** interact; a rhythmic figure, ♫♫|♩ 𝄾 ♫♫|♫♩♩|, which appears in a supporting role early in the movement plays an increasingly important part in the later action; the paired chords of **Ex. 18b** appear in numberless contexts and transformations. But the *legato* theme, **Ex. 20**, maintains its identity intact on each of its five appearances, appearing always in complete form and untransposed.

No final conclusions are reached; after the fifth appearance of **Ex. 20** on solo horn and an angry outburst from the full wind band, the movement ends peacefully in E minor with reminiscences of the rhythmic motive quoted above and a subdued comment from tubular bells.

The slow movement opens in D major with a solemn but sensuous tune for the strings, regularly structured in 4 + 4 + 4 + 6 phrases, and supported by romantic secondary-seventh harmony. In Mahler or Rachmaninov, such a tune could well have been subjected to far-reaching transformations, but Arnold never goes beyond the eighteen bars of his first statement, never varies the original harmonies, or presents his theme in any other key but its original D major:

Ex.21

Andante con moto (♩ = 69)

A calmer and more impersonal *legato* theme immediately follows, the use of low-register flute and high-register bassoon in unison giving an odd effect of disembodiment. It is at once repeated note for note and without transposition, first by oboe and trumpet in unison, then by the upper strings:*

Ex.22

Ex. 21 returns; a freely rhapsodic passage for violins in high intertwined counterpoint leads to a turbulent central episode based on fragmentary figures, after which action almost ceases as the various orchestral groups engage in a long drawn-out exchange of crescendo–diminuendo chords. After a further threefold statement of

---

*The reader is urged to read **Ex. 22** three times through at the speed of performance rather than gulping it down whole as quick score-readers are apt to do; this is one of those unspectacular tunes that depends for its effect on the deliberation with which the message is delivered and on the reinforcement of twofold repetition.

Ex. 22 the opening theme returns for the last time, in its original key and instrumentation.

The purposeful and compact third movement, one of the most forceful and individual of all his orchestral scherzos, bears many Arnold fingerprints. **Exx. 23a, b** and **c** show how closely the thematic material relates to that of the first movement:

Ex. 23a

Ex. 23b

Ex. 23c

Five-unit rhythms and ostinatos are thrown across the beat; lumbering canons for bass instruments call up visions of jostling elephants desperately hurrying to catch their trains. There are extreme, Berliozian contrasts of dynamic, abrupt shifts of tonality, daring juggling acts with massive blocks of orchestral masonry. D minor tonality at first predominates; later, there is a move towards B flat (somewhat obscured by inbuilt thematic chromaticisms) and a passage of over a hundred bars, with one sixteen-bar break, based on a C–G pedal that preludes the return to D minor (here and elsewhere, Arnold's use of a familiar expectation-raising device in no way guarantees an expectable resolution). In the final pages **Ex. 23c** appears in cross-beat augmentation, three crotchets in each 6/8 bar.

A ringing trumpet call heralds the main theme of the finale: an energetic dance-like tune set securely in B flat, scored for piccolos in 'horn harmony' with militaristic backing from side-drums and bass drums (note rhythmic figure **x** which plays an important part in later developments):

Ex.24a

Ex.24b

Once again we seem to be back in familiar Arnold country. But after a short fanfare passage based on **x**, the dance tune returns, this time undermined by contradictory and dissonant harmonies which dispose of the idea that all is to be sunshine and light. Woodwind skirls lead to a fierce and ungainly canonic episode for woodwind and brass (skirls and canon both derived **y** in **Ex. 24b**):

Ex.25a

Ex.25b

(continued)

Ex. 24b returns, again introduced by fanfare figures and military rhythms which persist in the background of a rambling tune for unison violins which declares its kinship with earlier themes. An extended and informal recapitulation follows in which all the tunes and motives so far heard play a part. Fanfares of increasing vehemence and a frantic bandying about of **Ex. 18c** lead to three tremendous chords on strings and lower wind (in fact, the first three chords of **Ex. 18b** taken in reverse):

Ex.26

In the ensuing tumult, the horn harmonies of the dance tune battle against fanfares and an ostinato based on **Ex. 25b**. Conflict abruptly ceases, and the opening theme of the first movement appears *fortissimo* on unison strings. The harmony tends towards D major, and after a massive eight-bar crescendo the emotional big theme of the slow movement sounds out, in its original D major, with its now familiar harmonic backing, and we prepare ourselves for a Franckian apotheosis.

But as the anticipated final cadence approaches, the harmony is wrenched around towards an inconsequent E major, then settles for E minor. There it sticks; tubular bells and timpani, as at the end of the first movement, quietly reaffirm the E minor chord, and the Symphony fades away on the cellos' and basses' low E.

I have perhaps harped too much on the ingenious processes of construction used in the Fifth Symphony, which (whatever the problems it sets the listener) certainly does not come over as laboured or intellectual music. At its first performance, it seems to have puzzled Arnold's former admirers and to have bewildered some critics, one of whom labelled it a study in disintegration – almost a compliment when we recall how many pioneering twentieth-century works have been condemned as chaotic or meaningless by contemporary commentators. It is true enough, however, that the Symphony has not the instant charm and attraction that characterizes many earlier Arnold works. The use of serial constructive methods has given a strange twist to some of the themes, while the big tune of the slow movement, which in the post-Grüber age most of us can take in our stride, spreads dismay in the severe and superior sixties.

Arnold himself had his doubts; his original semi-apologetic programme note remarked that 'the composer had failed to distinguish between sentiment and sentimentality' and that 'in times of great emotion we speak in emotional clichés'. Perhaps even the composer did not fully understand why such a tune should have forced its way into his Symphony. It has been suggested that its appearance in *fortissimo* apotheosis at the end of the last movement is satirical in intent. Yet the musical treatment it receives – or fails to receive – does nothing to support such a view. At most one might suggest that by repeating it always in identical form Arnold stresses its cliché character.

Apart from the big tune and the dance-like theme that comes in for such rough, bitonal handling in the finale, there are no memorable, Arnold-type melodies in the Symphony for the audience to whistle as it leaves the hall. It is the emotional tone as much as the contours of its themes or the character of its harmonies that makes the work both fascinating and disturbing.

9

THE SHAPING CONTEXT
Works for Special Occasions

Composers who can be relied on to produce lively and entertaining works to order as quickly as other men can write a letter will never lack commissions. For this reason, it was only to be expected that from an early stage in Arnold's career new pieces should have been in constant demand. What is at first sight more surprising is that he should have found time, in his busiest years, to write so many offbeat, special-occasion works which were never likely to enter the normal concert repertory.

But Arnold has always delighted in the challenge of new demands and new limitations and seems never to have turned down a commission that offered an escape route from the blander routines of concert life. From the first, he was much in sympathy with the spirit of misrule that prevailed at the Hoffnung Festivals, which made a huge joke out of many of our concert-going customs. The works composed for these Festivals were undertaken in a holiday spirit, but could also be taken as indirect protests at the solemn and narrow conventions of the age.

Among the most interesting and memorable of the special-occasion works are those in which the instrumental set-up allows least room for manoeuvre. *A Grand, Grand Overture* Op. 57, written in 1956 for the first of Gerard Hoffnung's concerts, includes three vacuum cleaners and one floor polisher in the score, as well as four riflemen. Hoovers were lending the vacuum cleaners and floor polisher, so that Arnold did not even have the choice of timbres and pitches between Hoover,

Electrolux, Goblin, and other noted vacuums of the day. He recognized, however, two vital factors in the musical set-up. First, that there was just one trick that this electronic quartet could effectively bring off: the building up, note by note, of what one must politely call a chord (a formula, possibly originating in the piled-up brass chords of the Overture to Borodin's *Prince Igor*, often used in expectation-rousing introductions and in film title music). Second, that the Hoover's dynamic power by no means equalled its suction power; the sound in a concert hall would be puny, and would add nothing to the *tuttis*. The quartet makes only three appearances in the overture, always against the lightest of accompaniments; altogether, the Hoovers are in action for fewer than 100 of the work's 429 bars. The riflemen fire eight shots in all, they too acting in follow-my-leader fashion.

After a brisk introduction the orchestra falls silent and the Hoovers sign on with a chord built up bar by bar, then held out for nine bars. No more is heard of them until the big tune, round which the whole overture is built, has been heard three times in varied instrumentations. After some byplay involving lively subsidiary figures, the Hoover chord returns, entries more widely spaced out at four-bar intervals and set against a *pizzicato* string figure. First violins enter with the main tune (*piano, espressivo*), two clarinets providing a harmonic counter-theme while the Hoovers repeat their one trick:

Ex. 1

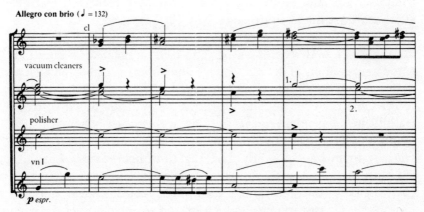

(continued)

The process is repeated freely in varied scoring, after which the Hoovers remain *tacet* until, just before the final *Vivace*, they sign off with a last unaccompanied chord, falling silent one by one.

The striking thing about the *Grand, Grand Overture* – apart from the character and memorability of the central tune – is that the composer treats his quartet of Hoovers with the same respect he would accord to instruments of the highest lineage, and by imaginative and sparing use conjures real music from them. Of course we laugh (and are meant to laugh) at the Hoovers; but we don't laugh at the expense of the music.

The United Nations and the *Grand Concerto Gastronomique* Op. 76, composed for later Hoffnung concerts, are both contrived around stage action, and in both cases Arnold was content to provide background music of an expectable, undistracting, variety. The most stirring event in *United Nations* was, in fact, un-notateable: after the bland deliberations of the UN Council and a short quodlibet in which national anthems intertwine harmoniously, four military bands entered and marched up and down the aisles of the Royal Festival Hall, their independent musics battling against each other. Arnold's hymn-like UN theme (which tails away in a much-repeated 'till-ready' pair of bars possibly deriving from Beethoven's *Egmont* Overture) is suitably decorous, and suitably anonymous. In the *Grand Concerto*, the storm music for *Oysters*, robust English tune for *Roast beef*, Italianate aria for *Peach Melba*, and so on, effectively bolster up the joke.

Leonora No. 4 (Beethoven–Strasse), composed for the final Hoffnung concert in 1961, is a more substantial musical joke. Here, Arnold leaves much of the spade work to Beethoven. For long stretches, the familiar *Leonora No. 3* pursues its accustomed course until some fresh disaster or incongruous musical happening causes disruption. Much play is made with the offstage trumpet, who can't wait for his cue, even making a tentative entry during the slow introduction. When the right moment comes and the strings land on their unison B flat, we wait hopefully, but nothing happens. The strings play the lead-in passage again, and this time trumpet fanfares sound out from every corner of the hall. There are cruder jokes as a brass band breaks in, first with a march, then with a waltz; also more subtle witticisms, as when the *Oberon* horn call is worked into the introduction so naturally that for a moment we wonder if that's where it really belongs. Arnold shows his skill as much in timing as in the manipulation of tones. After every unexpected happening, Beethoven is given long enough to draw us back into the music so that the next disruption is genuinely shocking.

Two of the six extra numbers added to Saint-Saëns's *Carnival of Animals* (Arnold's Op. 72) for the Hoffnung Memorial Concert of 1960 are straightforward joke pieces. *Jumbo* gives the *pizzicato* from Delibes's *Sylvia* to trombones and cellos, the trio section to tuba; in *Chiroptera* the whole orchestra silently mimes supersonic sounds. The other movements contain genuine and imaginative music. *The Giraffe* lopes along to a gawky 6/8, its head in the clouds; *Sheep* amble in canon on muted strings, *pianissimo*; *Cows* give a few glissando moos in a charming and placid pastorale; *Mice* have a tiny scherzo for treble instruments. The latter three in particular complement Saint-Saëns's portraits aptly and delightfully, and deserve to lead an independent musical life.

The *Toy Symphony* Op. 62 of 1957, scored for twelve toy instruments, piano and strings (or string quartet), was written to be performed by musician guests at a fund-raising dinner and is dedicated to the Musicians' Benevolent Fund. Arnold treats his toy instruments with as much respect as the Hoovers in *A Grand, Grand Overture*; the tunes are among his best, the mood is light-hearted but never frivolous, entirely appropriate to the original occasion. The *Toy Symphony* also stands up well as an independent work that can be played and listened to with enjoyment by musicians of any age on any informal musical occasion. As so often in Arnold's works, the medium and the message are one. It would be hard to account for the effect produced by the unassuming little tune of the last movement unless we took account of the instrumentation, spacing, and harmonic environment; divided violas chugging away far below; toy instruments (like the village bassoon in the scherzo of Beethoven's *Pastoral* Symphony) making, in all seriousness, their limited contribution; those sudden, shocking excursions to and from a remote C sharp minor. Once more, the ability to find the right home for a theme counts for as much as the character of the theme itself:

Ex. 2

Only a handful of those composers who have accepted radio commissions for abstract works rather than for incidental music have ever thought of adapting their concert-hall style to the acoustic or psychological circumstances of the studio broadcast – perhaps because no one has a clearly formulated notion of what those special circumstances are, perhaps because a studio broadcast of a commissioned work is optimistically regarded as a first step on the way to concert performance.

In the *Commonwealth Christmas Overture* Op. 64, commissioned by the BBC in 1957 for a programme celebrating the twenty-fifth anniversary of the first Christmas broadcast by a British monarch, Arnold followed the conventional course by using a standard symphony orchestra and scoring the music much in his habitual fashion. But the inclusion of a Caribbean episode for guitars, marimba, and Afro-Cuban percussion does suggest that he took note of the special circumstances. On the practical front, the BBC with its great resources would not have blenched at the thought of the extra players. The acoustic problems that might have arisen in the concert hall would also be reduced, since radio engineers can fit a symphony orchestra *plus* Jamaican pop group into the listener's sitting room as easily as a quartet, adjusting the balance as the broadcast proceeds. Nor would the sudden switch from Caribbean to concert music have disconcerted radio listeners, accustomed as they are to instant transitions at the push of a button.

The *Overture* begins (4/4 *Allegro giubiloso*) with rousing fanfares. One loses count of how many of Arnold's concert works and film scores open in this way – it is his most favoured 'way in' to a popular piece, comparable to the tonic-dominant assertions of eighteenth-century composers and the sweeping introductory flourishes of the harpist. But in this case, the extended theme that follows digests the fanfares into its own substance, so that they form an integral part of the work. A second, lighter and jauntier theme follows, provocatively flaunting its glissandos. The tempo changes to 3/4 *Allegretto* for what sounds like the 'big theme' we expect at the succulent centre of a popular overture. But before it can develop its full potential, the Caribbean music breaks in, and the orchestra (except for the double-basses) falls silent. Guitars lead the dance; trumpets and trombone, then flute, join in for a few bars. At last, the whole orchestra rises up and overwhelms the Caribbean group, who are heard no more. A shortened recapitulation of the *Allegro giubiloso* brings the *Overture* to an end.

Like those eighteenth-century composers who employ different styles in divertimenti, operas, church music and chamber works, Arnold will regularly vary the communicative register according to the occasion. For the connoisseurs at the St Cecilia Dinner, he had turned out an almost classical little chamber symphony, in which humour was incidental to music. A commission to write a work for the Last Night of the Proms in 1970 gave rise to the Fantasy for Audience and Orchestra, a 'public' work designed to appeal to the most innocent and unsophisticated music-lovers. In this case, the Last Night revellers in the Royal Albert Hall were surely more in Arnold's thoughts than the huge audience of radio listeners.

The main section of the Fantasy is built around the protest song 'We shall overcome', which could hardly be performed at a Prom in the 1980s without diligent preliminary rehearsal, but which in 1970 was familiar to everyone under the age of twenty-five, its popularity due partly to simplicity and singability, partly to sentiments that are bold and inspiring but vague enough to commit the singer to no specific political or activist viewpoint.

Arnold gave the audience six verses to sing, accompanying the voices with conventional harmonies of basic simplicity. The performance provided no treats for passive listeners; but Promenaders can't have too much of a good thing, and the experience proved to be as exhilarating for those involved as the mass performances of 'Jerusalem' or 'Rule Britannia' (which puts in a brief appearance at the end of the Fantasy).

The work opens with an expectation-rousing introduction for full orchestra; the first two verses of the protest song follow, then a scherzo interlude for woodwind and harp. After verse 4 comes a fanfare interlude for brass and percussion, these episodes giving the orchestra opportunities for display and the performing audience a chance to draw breath.

Next comes Arnold's 5/8 version of the traditional hornpipe, well known to all Promenaders from Henry Wood's *Fantasia on British Sea Songs*, which the BBC were at this time hoping to banish from the Last Night programme:

Ex.3

This cock-eyed variation gave the Promenaders a rhythm worth stamping the feet to, at the same time wonderfully enlivening a hackneyed tune. The crooked hornpipe comes off so well that one wishes Arnold had more often experimented, Bernstein-wise, with the less familiar metres.

Unlike other composers who were commissioned round about this time for Last Night works, Arnold had no trouble in tuning in to the Promenaders' wavelength. In terms of audience response, the Fantasy must have been one of the most successful of all Proms commissions. It was, however, little approved by a number of critics who censured Arnold for playing down to the masses. Arnold might reasonably have been accused of encouraging the rowdier elements in the audience and making nonsense of the BBC's wish to raise the tone of the celebrations, and no doubt took this course deliberately, judging the Last Night to be no occasion for musical refinements or subtleties. The Fantasy is more of a musical poster than a polished concert work, in workmanship more akin to the rapidly written film scores than to the symphonies and concertos. Significantly (perhaps even defiantly?) he introduces the protest song with the most ancient and banal of music-hall clichés:

Ex.4

The Fantasies for Solo Wind Instruments were composed for a very different occasion and for a very different audience, having been commissioned for the Birmingham International Wind Competition of 1966 to be played, in the first instance, to a select panel of judges. The original set of five (for flute, oboe, clarinet, bassoon and horn) abound in the sort of brilliant and showy passages that find no place in the Sonatinas of earlier years. No need, however, to assume that Arnold's views of instrumental characters had changed; it was the occasion that shaped the music.

To serve its function, each piece has to test the player's facility in rapid passage-work in all registers, powers of endurance, command of every sort of articulation, ability to sustain a solemn *adagio* melody even when it follows a hurtling flight of *staccato* notes. Arnold's business is not to indulge instruments in their favourite tricks; thus, the Fantasy for Bassoon Op. 86 includes no characteristic (and easy-to-bring-off) wide-leaping passages, but finger-twisting chromaticisms, rapid scales and arpeggios that don't proceed in predictable sequences as in the books of studies. In the Fantasy for Horn Op. 88, the instrument is tested by a slur from d through d' to d'' (and preceded by an A) that would be more taxing for many players than some of the far more acrobatic *vivace* passages.

Each is a self-contained entity bound together by thematic cross-connections. All are in some sort of cyclic form. In the Fantasy for Oboe Op. 90 the first phrase of the opening *Allegretto* returns after a short independent *Vivace* section to provide material for the central *Andante con moto*, making another appearance at the end of the work. The rhetorical opening theme of the Fantasy for Clarinet Op. 87 is later transformed into an *Alla marcia*. The Fantasies call for players of high technical skills, and in fact Arnold did not underestimate the capacities of the competitors. The winner in the oboe class was Maurice Bourgue, in the flute class, James Galway.

In 1969, Arnold wrote an additional set of fantasies for trumpet, trombone and tuba. The Fantasy for Trumpet Op. 100 is dedicated to Ernest Hall, the teacher whom he most loved and admired at the RCM. This fantasy also contains taxing scales and arpeggios over the instrument's full range; but it is noble as well as brilliant, opening with a long paragraph of freely organised melody which seems to encapsulate the performing character of one of the finest of our 'straight' trumpeters of the 30s, 40s and 50s (the later Concerto gives another picture of trumpet character, partly, no doubt, because it was

written for John Wilbraham, a player with a style of his own). Though
Arnold never takes the instrument up to Mahlerian heights, the
Fantasy is still a great test of a player's stamina; there are just three
quavers' rest in the first 70 bars of 4/4 *Allegro energico* and 6/8 *Vivace.*

Arnold's view of trombone character is less orthodox. It is only in
the brief central *Andante* of the Fantasy for Trombone Op. 101 that we
hear the 'noble instrument' in sustained middle-register *legato.* The
Fantasy opens with a frantic and grotesque 6/8 *Allegro* ($\downarrow$=112)
encompassing huge leaps and abrupt dynamic changes; after the
Andante comes an equally hectic *Allegro* 2/4 ($\downarrow$=126) with tongued
semiquaver chromatic scales and arpeggios calling for almost
superhuman agility. In painting this portrait of the trombone at its
wildest and most ferocious, Arnold seems for once to have moved
from the realm of the practical into the realm of the ideal. I've not yet
heard the work live, but hear that there are intrepid performers who
have successfully achieved public performance.

The Fantasy for Tuba Op. 102 begins and ends with a minuet-like
Grazioso which well displays the urbane side of the instrument's
character. The player then exercises violently in a brief 6/8
Allegro, Arnold allowing him many of those spectacular leaps he
denied to the bassoon. The minuet returns, to be followed by a
restless and *legato Andante con moto* guaranteed to leave the player
gasping for breath, before the minuet is recapitulated for the last time.
In his orchestral works Arnold has often shown willingness to treat
the tuba sympathetically, even poetically, as a solo instrument, but I
don't think that in this case he expects us to take it too seriously as
graceful dancer, acrobat, or master of *bel canto.*

Another test piece, the Fantasy for Brass Band Op. 114(a), was written
for the National Championships in 1974 and received its first nineteen
performances in the Royal Albert Hall before an expert audience of
bandsmen, many of them armed with piano-conductor scores.
Arnold, alert as ever to the special needs of a special occasion, came
up with a lively work designed to test the strengths and weaknesses
of the nineteen best bands in the country. The Fantasy is very much in
the traditional brass-band idiom, with appealing tunes nestling

among the fanfares, virtuoso scale flurries, solemn interludes in full harmony and the inevitable and necessary cornet solos. In mood and idiom, the Fantasy has little in common with the later Symphony for Brass Instruments; Arnold writes on the (justifiable) assumption that brass-band and symphonic players inhabit different worlds of music, and provides each with music tailored to their tastes and requirements. But the *incipit* of the Fantasy's cornet solo does appear, unchanged, in the later Trumpet Concerto (see p.206). A tribute, perhaps, both to the sweet and fluent style of the best cornet players and to the trumpeters who, in the post-war years, had learned a few lessons from them.

Of the many fanfares Arnold has provided for special occasions the longest and most remarkable is the *Fanfare for Louis* written to celebrate Louis Armstrong's seventieth birthday in 1970. The two trumpets involved compete with brilliant triplet and semiquaver repeated-note figures rather as the great jazz trumpeters once competed in the streets of New Orleans, play follow-my-leader games with angular seventh motives, and occasionally join in forceful unisons. A brief *Maestoso* interlude serves as slow movement to this compact but eventful work.

Early in his career Arnold wrote a number of short piano pieces designed for young pianists in the earliest stage. These are conventional in tunes and harmonies and are carefully devised to lie nicely under the fingers, but are curiously anonymous in style; the piano has never been one of the instruments that inspired Arnold to strikingly fresh or personal invention. But the Duo for Two Cellos Op. 85, commissioned for a teaching book and composed in 1965, is a charming and characteristic work, skilfully laid out for players of limited technique, composed to length to fill a double spread. Materials are simple: a lyrical motive based on thirds, one of Arnold's favoured rocking figures. Action is shared out equitably, with many contrasts of *arco* and *pizzicato*; there is a hint of bitonality. The Duo is one of those bagatelles, slight in itself, which declares its maker's fine craftsmanship and grasp of the issues involved as clearly as any fifty-minute symphony.

10

MAN FOR ALL SEASONS
Concert Works 1962–75

There are periods in Arnold's life when it is as pointless to attempt an evolutionary approach to the music as it would be in the case of Berlioz. During the sixties and seventies he fulfilled commissions from some of the most distinguished performers in the country, at the same time becoming increasingly involved in amateur music-making, while offbeat commissions led him to explore much new ground. It was a period of unsettlement and stress in his own life, and of diversification in his music. A few signposts point forward toward the more openly expressive and darker-hued works that were to follow; but it is hard to discern any fixed focus or steady line of development, while occasional pieces such as the Fantasies for Solo Wind Instruments and the *Padstow Lifeboat March* defy attempts to establish their musical heredity.

The Five Pieces for Violin and Piano Op. 84, written in 1964 as encore pieces for Yehudi Menuhin, reflect his character as a violinists as well as the breadth of his musical interests. The *Prelude* (4/4 *Con energico*) pays tribute to Vivaldi, opening flamboyantly with a fine violinistic flourish rising from G string to the heights, the piano supplying an equally strong counter-theme:

Ex. 1

(continued)

The violin briefly explores the lyrical potential of the opening figure before the twinned themes return. An *Aubade* follows; unlike most of its dreamy species, this is a light-footed scherzo (6/8 *Vivace*) freely based on an Indian raga and characterized by flattened second and raised fourth degrees. Next comes a tiny *Waltz* (3/4 *Grazioso*) with a touch of parody in its neatly turned gestures, soulful chromaticisms and *deux-temps* rhythms. The fourth piece, which derives from the ballet *Rinaldo and Armida*, is a *Ballad* (4/4 *Andantino*), and takes itself quite seriously. A sustained and expressive violin melody is repeated in the upper octave note for note over plain and expectable syncopated harmonies. There are unobtrusive subtleties in the tune itself: back-references to the rising third of the opening (F sharp, G sharp, A) and a 6 + 8 bar structure agreeably disorientates the listener at the midway mark. The last piece is a *Moto perpetuo* (2/2 *Presto*) 'based on the type of phrases first used by Charlie Parker'. A slippery, eel-like tune, **Ex. 2a**, contradicts the pounding bass beat with cross-rhythms and syncopations, finally exploding in a firework burst of cadential flourishes, **Ex. 2b**:

Ex. 2a

Ex. 2b

Although designed to be played separately, the five pieces (keynotes D, E, G, F sharp, D) form a nicely varied suite in which Arnold shows us how unselfconsciously he can slip into some already clearly defined idiom without compromising his own character.

The Fantasy for Guitar Op. 107 was written for Julian Bream and first performed by him in London in May 1971. Bream has edited the Fantasy, mapping the player's course very precisely with explanations of the special techniques and symbols used. The work runs through without a break. While the idiom is a little more severe than that of the Concerto, the Fantasy is both virtuosic and tuneful, likely to stimulate performers of the first class and to give pleasure to non-specialist listeners as well as to *afficionados* of guitar playing.

First comes a toccata-like *Prelude* (4/4 *Maestoso*): ringing seventh chords are superimposed on a timpani-like bass pedal on A and E; a central section spells out related seventh harmonies in arpeggios. A *Scherzo* (6/8 *Allegro*) deals in brilliant repeated-note figures, with a slower-moving central section in which Arnold unostentatiously deploys three twelve-tone rows and one that narrowly misses twelve-tone perfection. A four-sectioned *Arietta* (3/4 *Andante con moto*) is of straightforward $A-A_1-A-A$ form, the whole movement consisting of four near-repeats of an eight-bar tune with a two-bar coda. A short *Fughetta* draws material for its central episode from the arpeggios of the *Prelude*. A second *Arietta* (9/8 *Semplice e languido*) makes telling use of third-based harmony and artificial harmonics, and leads to a *March* based on the guitar's 'snare-drum' effect. This leads direct and without change of tempo into a free recapitulation of the trio section of the *Scherzo*, thence to a *Postlude* in which the material of the opening *Prelude* is reworked.

The *Trevelyan Suite* Op. 96 was written in 1967 for the opening of Trevelyan College at the University of Durham, and is scored for the instruments available at the university – hence the unusual ensemble of three flutes, two each of oboes, clarinets and horns with a single cello. (Arnold has however authorized the use of two bassoons in place of the cello.) Three very short movements together form hardly more than an extended ceremonial flourish. The opening Palindrome makes good use of crisp wind-band *staccato*; only one or two odd offbeat chords give the compositional game away. The central *Nocturne* is led by solo cello (its promising theme is cut short, seemingly before it has fulfilled its destiny, as though Arnold was aware that he mustn't keep the visiting celebrities waiting too long). The final *Apotheosis* is suitably grand and emphatic, with a brilliant episode for twinned clarinets, echoed by flutes, in Arnold's liveliest vein.

The Concerto for 28 Players, commissioned by the Stuyvesant Foundation and first performed by the English Chamber Orchestra in May 1970 under Arnold's direction, is scored for one flute, two oboes, one bassoon and two horns with twelve violins, four violas, four cellos and two double-basses. Violins are regularly divided *a 6*, with solo parts for two first and two second violins, while the back two desks of firsts and seconds play throughout in unison, dividing only for the occasional chord.

The Concerto is a chamber-music rather than a virtuoso work, not calling for spectacular technical skills but demanding finesse in ensemble playing – the intricate counterpoint of the first *Vivace* and the close-knotted canons of first and second movements could all too easily sound dense and muddy with less than first-rank players. The Concerto also seems to presuppose a sophisticated audience able to pick up hidden clues and allusions, while the opening chords issue a warning: 'If you don't like sharply flavoured harmony, leave this work alone.'

Ex.3a

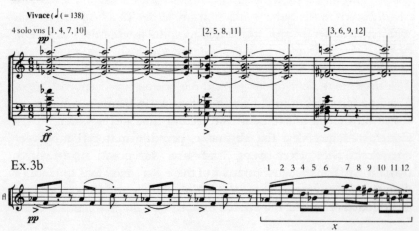

Ex.3b

Ex.3c

Ex.3d

The first movement opens with three wide-spaced chords, **10:3a**, accented but dodging the beat in Stravinskyan manner, which recur thrice during the movement (the second time in the order 2–3–1). Contrasted motives, **Ex. 3b** and **c**, provide material for lively conversational exchanges and are subjected to various transformations: the most complex of these is a canon that combines **x** with its own augmentation, **Ex. 3d**. Note too the connection between the three chords and the twelve-tone row of **Ex. 3b**, chord 1 being

formed from the four first notes of each triplet group, chord 2 from
the second notes, chord 3 from the third. x takes on a new expressive
character in augmentation, supported by the three chords of **Ex. 3a**:

Ex.4

There are further affinities with Stravinsky in the angular themes,
staccato quaver accompaniment figures, metrical patterns that conflict
with the regular 6/8 metre, idiosyncratic chord spacing, and more
generally in the ingenuity and dry wit that characterize the whole
work. The unselfconscious mixing of atonal and tonal elements is,
however, special to Arnold. It is worth noting, as a tiny sign of his
instinct for the practical and effective, that the more convoluted
atonal figures appear only at moderate tempi; all semiquaver
passages are based on simple diatonic figures that lie comfortably
under the fingers.

The slow movement (3/4 *Larghetto*) is based on two contrasted
themes, one serial and fragmented, **Ex. 5a**, the other tonal, song-like,
developing as a broad band of four-part harmony, **Ex. 5b**:

Ex.5a

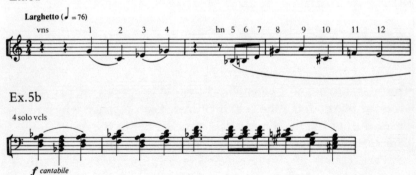

Ex.5b

Ex.5c

Ex. 5a is volatile and liable to transformation, giving rise, in six-part close canon, to an atmospheric and Bartókian blur of sound. Two further transformations are shown at Ex. 5c. Ex. 5b retains its identity on each of its three appearances (all on divided cellos). Rhythmic figures derived from both themes play an important unifying role.

The last movement (2/4 *Allegro*) is in A–B–A–C–A form, a brisk little march with two trios, the middle entry of the main theme being condensed to a terse eight bars.

Ex.6

(continued)

The march theme is shown above with the counterpoint added at its first repetition. The notes of the wind are prolonged by solo violins to form quiet background chords (both theme and treatment recall the opening of the last movement of the Fifth Symphony, **Ex. 24a**, of Chapter 8 (p. 119). Trio 1 is introduced by horn fanfares in E flat over an E flat marching bass which persists throughout the section. But the swinging tune that appears after the horns' introductory twelve bars is in E major (later moving to F major):

Ex.7

In this context and in strange harmonic perspective, a tune that would be happily at home in brass- or military-band circles takes on the character of a visitor from another planet – its appearance more than a little reminiscent of the odd incursion of the robust hymn tune 'I vow to thee, my country' into Holst's *Jupiter*.

There are further surprises in store in the second trio. The brief return of the march theme is followed by two alternating cluster chords for much-divided violas and double-basses, repeated many times in *pianissimo*. Against these, at wide-spaced intervals of time, upper strings project short *fortissimo* phrases derived from the march theme:

Ex.8

The process is reversed, with cluster chords on solo violins and oboes, the *fortissimo* phrases on lower strings and horns, after which the march returns, *tutti fortissimi* and rushes quickly to an abrupt and unexpected D major conclusion.

Concertos

The Concerto for Two Violins and String Orchestra Op. 77, commissioned by Yehudi Menuhin and first performed by Menuhin and Albert Lysy at the Bath Festival in 1962, bears certain obvious resemblances to the famous Bach double concerto. Both are based in contrapuntal dialogue, with the orchestra involved in the action almost on equal terms with the soloists, the main motives being freely discussed by solo and *ripieno* strings. The soloists converse between themselves as equals and are much involved in follow-my-leader pursuits, the second player sometimes pressing close on the heels of the first, sometimes echoing a phrase at many bars' distance. In both cases, a serene and spacious slow movement is flanked by vigorous *allegros*.

Stylistically, the Concerto is one of the most consistent of Arnold's works, classical in form and idiom rather than neo-classical, a term that generally implies, if not self-consciousness, a keen awareness of the gulf separating eighteenth and twentieth centuries. Arnold never gives us the feeling that he is tightly armoured in 'a style', or putting on any sort of special act, or behaving in any way out of character. As in his jazz- and pop-orientated works, he writes from within the idiom even though in this case he stretches it far beyond eighteenth century limits.

At the same time, I doubt whether many would spot the composer without pre-knowledge or a fairly detailed study of the score. Catchy tunes are conspicuous by their absence (and would be out of place when interest centres on processes rather than themes). In a work that traces its lineage to Vivaldi and Bach, there are none of those abrupt modulations or changes of mood in which Arnold specializes. The 'quality' of the concerto lies in the freedom and variety of invention, in the composer's command of the developing situation and precise sense of what can, and cannot, be achieved within the rules of this particular game. It is characteristic of Arnold that there should be no dogged following through of merely ingenious contrapuntal processes to the point of tedium, no puritanical shunning of violinistic 'effect'. As in many of Bach's finest contrapuntal movements, there are relatively few 'ingenuities' in the Concerto in the form of augmentations, inversions, multiple canons, and the like. The next example shows some of the ways in which material is handled: a) imitative voices merging to form a compound melody; b) the orchestral transformation of the same material; c) contrapuntal bravura; and d) violin parts (in a passage from the final *Vivace)* which could, considered in isolation, induce a sort of tonal vertigo; but the apparent contradictions resolve themselves when we take into account the orderly motion of the bass.

Ex.9a

Ex.9b

Ex.9c

Ex.9d

(continued)

The Concerto for Two Pianos (Three Hands) and Orchestra Op. 104
was commissioned by the BBC for the 1969 Proms, and is dedicated
'To Phyllis and Cyril with affection and admiration'. Cyril Smith, who
had lost the use of his left hand after suffering a stroke in 1956, had
since built up a new career playing three-handed duos with his wife
Phyllis Sellick; Arnold was one of several British composers who
contributed to their specialized repertory.

Ravel, Prokofiev, and Britten had performed prodigies of ingenuity
in laying out the piano parts of their left-hand concertos so as to
establish the soloist in self-sufficient virtuosity. In this more
companionable duo-concerto, the one-handed pianist shares the load
with his partner. There is a risk that his limitations may be exposed
more obviously when he plays in conjunction with a two-handed
pianist, but Arnold gets over this problem in various ways. Neither
player is given much in the way of virtuoso passages, so that
comparisons need not be made. In this, Arnold is only following his
usual custom in writing for the piano – ingenious and elaborate
pianistic devices have never been in his line; the piano remains for
him something of a utility instrument, given to plain and direct
statement, steering clear of the elegant sophistications of
pianist–composers.

For much of the time, he treats the duo as a single, three-handed
unit. There is little sharing out of material; where either pianist has a
theme, the partner falls silent or supplies supporting harmony or

decorative counter-themes. Arnold reserves one particular trick for the exclusive use of the one-handed pianist: the presentation of a theme in tremolo. This device, over-exploited and cheapened by nineteenth-century drawing-room composers, has been shunned by serious twentieth-century composers, or used only in a spirit of parody (as in Weill's *Mahaganny*). In Arnold's rowdy, jazzy finale, it is once more treated as a legitimate and respectable technique, the zither-like sounds perfectly in place, pleasantly and freshly shocking.

The overall layout of this short and cheerful work is simple. All three movements are in A–B–A form; in the first and last movements the B section is songful, the outer sections lively and rumbustuous, and in the middle movement the process is reversed. The first (4/4 *Allegro moderato*) opens with a bold clattering *tutti* (A) in which the pianos play a *concertante* role while descending scales in the bass affirm the rock-solid C major tonality. A seductive theme in sixths of uncertain tonality (B) is introduced by the single-handed pianist (Piano I) and taken up by the flutes. Quiet reminiscences of the opening *tutti* lead to an exact repetition of the *legato* theme on Piano I and a recapitulation of the opening section.

The main eight-bar theme of the second movement (3/4 *Andante con moto*) is a gentle waltz-like *cantabile*, given in turn to Piano I, Piano II, and strings, the pianists branching off into ornamental counter-themes once the theme has been stated, so that at the second repeat the theme is enmeshed in two layers of decorative counterpoint. A turbulent and non-thematic central episode intervenes before two further repetitions of the main theme, which at its final entry returns to its simplest form, stripped of accompanying counter-themes. This increase and decline of textural complexity creates an arch form of its own, so that the five repetitions of an eight-bar theme over unvaried harmony (plus one rude interruption) do in fact add up to a slight but shapely movement.

The final 2/2 *Allegro* creates a rowdy, jazz-orientated setting for one of Arnold's 'big tunes', the syncopated and disjointed themes and circus rhythms of its first and last sections creating a mood of hectic gaiety, with many passing conflicts of tonality. Slippery chromatic figures, oompah basses and blues-like ambiguities abound. The big tune itself, with its many built-in repeats, is shared between Piano I

and strings; it is one of the most vigorous and infectious 'popular'
tunes Arnold has ever composed:

Ex. 10

Concerto No. 2 for Flute and Orchestra Op. 111 is a work of the same
species as the First Flute Concerto (composed nineteen years earlier)
and likewise dedicated to Richard Adeney. It is lightly scored for a
Mozartian orchestra of strings with oboes and horns. The first

movement is again *Allegro*; but *moderato* rather than *vivace*. Once more, long, flowing themes alternate with lively and brilliant passage-work in upper registers. Again, Arnold makes virtually no use of the flute's dark and sensuous lower register. The main themes are once more characterized by long appoggiaturas which yield late to the underlying harmony, and which give a sort of pathos to many of the flute's more expressive phrases, **Ex. 11a**. The little fanfare figure that crops up later is (in context) anything but jubilant, the gesture of one who whistles to keep his spirits up, **Ex. 11b**:

Ex.11a

Ex.11b

The second movement (9/8 *Vivace*) is a lively scherzo in A–B–A form, **Ex. 12a** developing from a dance-like *staccato* phrase in Phrygian E minor (the second degree of the scale being flattened), the sustained melody of **Ex. 12b** providing contrast (note the rhythmic figure in the piano part carried over from the flute's first theme):

Ex.12a

Ex.12b

The hint of a whole-tone scale at x is a little Debussyan, and indeed the wistful, searching mood of the whole Concerto is not unlike that of the late Debussy sonatas, in which cello or violin hunt among the debris of classical practices for new characters, new purposes. Nor is the final *Allegretto* more reassuring; a hesitating waltz, in which once again the long appoggiatura features largely, the key phrase of **Ex. 13** recurring in identical form ten times during this three-minute movement. The effect is cumulative, as in those Tchaikovsky slow movements where some expressive phrase carries its own invariable yearning harmony which gains in pathos at each repetition:

Ex. 13

The Concerto for Viola and Chamber Orchestra Op. 108 was commissioned by the Northern Sinfonia Orchestra for its then principal viola Roger Best with funds from Northern Arts, and was first performed in October 1971. The problem of writing a full-scale concerto for such a retiring instrument had been previously approached in various ways. Hindemith in his *Kleine Kammermusik No. 5* for solo viola and chamber ensemble reduced the viola to the status of a *concertante* instrument, its part woven into a contrapuntal web of great complexity. Walton, in his Concerto, freed the orchestra from subservience in extended *tuttis* the viola becoming the leading actor in the drama rather than the musical supremo of convention. In both these works, for obvious reasons, predominating use is made of upper registers, and as a result we are given a partial view of viola character. Arnold, by contrast, writes freely in all registers, and we are made aware of the viola's wide variety of timbres and of the ways in which themes may be transformed when heard on different strings and at different pitches. The orchestra used is not large (one flute, two each of oboes, clarinets, bassoons and horns, with strings), scoring is light, textures clear; in no other viola concerto can there be so few occasions on which the soloist is seen labouring away at passages that may have taken weeks to master but that are almost inaudible to the listener. Except for one short octave passage at the end of the last movement, there are in fact no technical problems that would worry a player able to cope with the orchestral viola parts in Wagner and Strauss.

The first movement (2/4 *Allegro con spirito*) opens in resonant E minor with vigorous arpeggio and scale figures in a long paragraph organized in sequential patterns and covering the whole of the instrument's 'normal' range (**Ex. 14a**); x and y are to play important roles in later developments:

Ex. 14a

Ex.14b

solo va

p

The orchestra plays an unobtrusive supporting part, only the bassoons (in thirds) being briefly involved in thematic interplay. The solo viola also announces the long, song-like B minorish theme that immediately follows (the opening is shown at **Ex. 14b**). The forty-bar tune is at once repeated, shadowed in double canon by solo flute and clarinet, over the lightest syncopated accompaniment. The orchestra is more actively involved in a fantasia section largely based on **Ex. 14a**, towards the end of which the viola weaves free arabesques above **Ex. 14b**, reminiscing on motives from the first paragraph. Recapitulation is virtually a *d a capo* of the two opening sections.

The slow movement is a rondo ($A–B–C_1–A–C_2–A$), the episodes including some development and some new material. The sombre theme is qualified by contradictory dissonances:

Ex.15a

Andante con moto (♩ = 72)

Once again, the viola leads throughout the exposition section (of thirty-five bars), adding a freely dissonant and more rhapsodic

counter-theme as the bassoons and lower strings take over the first
theme:

Ex.15b

Developments based on x and a diminution of the main theme follow;
the viola introduces a second theme of the same family, later to be
treated in triple canon:

Ex.15c

Ex.15d

The final 6/8 *Allegro vivace* opens with vigorous and rapidly
modulating two-part contrapuntal exchanges, viola versus orchestra,
followed by a genial *cantabile* theme for the soloist securely founded
on an A major sumer-is-icumen-in ostinato in the bass:

Ex.16

The new theme and the orchestra's comments thereon contain several references to first-movement motives (compare the descending chromatic figure in the last bar of **Ex. 16** with **y** in **Ex. 14a**). Arnold plays around with the major–minor thirds without rousing memories of Walton's regretful, bitter-sweet use of the same harmonic complex in his Viola Concerto. This movement never lingers or looks back, but moves briskly and cheerfully onwards, recapitulating earlier sections in reverse order. When the ostinato section returns in C major, the soloist accompanies the violins' **Ex. 16** with a prolonged flourish of arpeggios – not of the elaborate and sophisticated sort of the advanced study books, but in lowest positions and using the resonant open strings to produce a thick band of viola sound which forms only one of several elements in the final orchestral *tutti*.

Music for Orchestra

By the late sixties, Arnold was widely known as a composer capable of the grand gesture, whose music was at the same time tuneful, cheerful, relatively uncomplicated, always effective in performance. It was only to be expected that, among the commissions that came his way, a number should be for works for joyful occasions. Yet the three overtures of this period suggest that something in his nature was rebelling against the idea of producing an endless stream of jubilant, affirmative pieces to order. Even the early *Beckus*, it is true, had undercurrents of unease; but there had been a cheerful recklessness about the music that spoke of a high-spirited composer swimming buoyantly with the tide. The main themes of *Peterloo* and *The Fair Field*, neither carefree nor jubilant in character, belong in another category, while the perorations of all three, grandiose but a little perfunctory, suggest that Arnold himself may have been going through the motions of celebration in less than whole-hearted fashion. Significantly, the most memorable passage in the three overtures is the 'black' central episode in *Peterloo*: musical poster-painting of deliberate crudity and savagery, which goes far beyond the conventional limits of picturesque illustration.

Peterloo Op. 97 was commissioned by the Trades Union Congress to celebrate the centenary of the first meeting of the TUC in 1868 and was first performed at the Royal Festival Hall in London on 7 June 1968. It is one of the few concert works written to a specific programme, the music depicting the massacre at St Peter's Fields, Manchester, on 16 August 1819, when (as a note in the score tells us) 'an orderly crowd of some 8000 people met to hear a speech on political reform. On the orders of the magistrates they were interrupted by the Yeomanry . . . Cavalry were sent in, eleven people were killed and four hundred injured in the ensuing panic.'

The Overture, itself in A–B–A form, opens quietly with an A–B–A theme. The A section is made up of 4 + 4 + 4 + 4 bars for unison strings, with trombones, tuba, harp and basses supplying conventional harmonies; the eight-bar B section is scored for woodwind with harp. The first eight bars of A give a fair idea of the mood and character of this *nobile* tune, half hymn, half song:

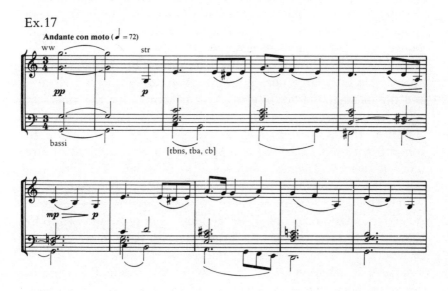

Ex.17

Soon after the seventh bar of the reprise of A we become aware of an ominous duple-time percussion rhythm (two side-drums and bass drum) sounding through the hymn-song. The peaceful tune halts indecisively on a foreign harmony as the military rapidly approach (eight bars from *pianissimo* to *forte*), and we are into the B section of the Overture.

This is based on a variety of short and ferocious motives: insistent percussion rhythms, snarls from the brass, short fragments of march-like nature from the trombones, tuba, and lower strings in passages reminiscent of the march episode in the Fourth Symphony finale. The time signature of 4/4 gives way to 6/8 – the traditional rhythm for galloping cavalry. Successive motives on trumpets, timpani, woodwind and strings make play with the diminished fifth (*diabolus in musica*); the music passes through many phases of fury (all in *fortissimo*) until at last, after a rapid *accelerando*, a *fortissimo* tam-tam stroke stills the tumult and initiates a short funeral march (4/4 *Lento*) led by percussion, with sombre chromatic comments from lower instruments. The solo oboe leads back into the B section of the opening theme, and the complete A–B–A paragraph follows, now in G major, the final reprise of A slowing to *maestoso*, and an *1812*-like climax with the main theme supported by rushing string scales, tubular bells and glockenspiel joining in the last triumphant assertion of G major.

The occasion had called for something bold and simple, appreciable by a large non-specialist (even non-musical) audience, and the message is forcefully put over in terms even the tone-deaf could hardly mistake. Arnold works through a whole vocabulary of warlike clichés in depicting senseless brutality, refusing to compliment the Cavalry by equipping them with motives of any intrinsic interest. Themes count for little, but there is considerable skill in the way in which the forces of evil are stage-managed, and in which episode succeeds episode so that impetus is never lost. Arnold's scenario does not allow the motives of good and evil to be brought into direct conflict; the brutal Cavalry have things all their own way, and there can be no interaction as in Beethoven's *Battle of Vittoria* or Tchaikovsky's *1812*. Probably for this reason, the return of the *nobile* theme comes as something of an anticlimax – it has been nowhere, experienced nothing, since we first met it, and there seems no good musical reason why it should sail home in G major triumph.

The *Anniversary Overture* Op. 99 of 1968 (originally the *Hong Kong Anniversary Overture*) was written for the twenty-first anniversary of the Hong Kong Philharmonic Society. Writing for an orchestra of uncertain quality, Arnold produced a short and straightforward work in a now familiar format that makes few demands on players or listeners. A bold and bracing first theme rising by fourths from C through F' and B flat' to E flat', its main rhythmic figure is fanfare-ized by the brass, a more song-like second theme in E flat built up from four similar four-bar phrases, falling sequentially. Both themes are repeated in varied forms, the first being briefly treated in augmentation, the Overture ending with a recapitulation of both themes in the home key of F.

The Overture *The Fair Field*, commissioned to celebrate the tenth anniversary of the opening of Fairfield Hall, Croydon, was first performed there in April 1973. *The Fair Field* consists in essence of a free-developing waltz section followed by a *galop* based on the same thematic material – a formal pattern similar to that of Sullivan's *Di Ballo* Overture. In Germany it would probably be known as the 'Thirds' Overture: the waltz-like opening theme and its two most important subsidiary themes are both patterned in thirds; euphonious third-based harmony founded in root-position seventh chords prevails throughout:

Ex.18a

Much of the first, main section of the Overture is in clearly defined waltz rhythm. Tunes and motives, and particularly the head-motive **x** of **Ex. 18a**, are fragmented, combined, subjected to simple transformation processes, the waltz theme (**Ex. 18a**) itself being at last transformed into a brisk 2/4 *galop*.

A solo trumpet plays an exuberant variation on **Ex. 18b**, **x** giving rise to a violent bitonal dispute between rival sections of the full orchestra, and leading back to 3/4 and a grandiose resumption of **Ex. 18a**, *lento e maestoso*.

Sinfonietta No. 3 Op. 81, completed in September 1964 and first performed by the New Philharmonia Orchestra in January 1965, is scored for one flute, two oboes, two bassoons, two horns, and strings. While the earlier Sinfoniettas could have been conceived as twentieth-century equivalents of the eighteenth-century divertimento, No. 3 is conspicuously lacking in the easy-going or boisterously affirmative diatonic tunes that Arnold once provided so generously. The harmonic atmosphere is generally unsettled, chromaticisms being built into both tunes and harmonies.

The two themes from the first movement (3/4 *Allegro vivace*) shown below belong very much to Arnold's later period. Note the austere harmonies of **Ex. 19a**, the reiterating of matching two-bar phrases, and the restricted pitch range. **Ex. 19b** shows the answering phrase; a canonic theme in four interweaving voices in which the melodic strands form part of a single unity:

Ex. 19a   Third Sinfonietta

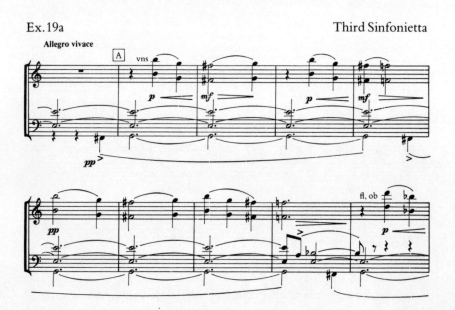

Ex.19b

The second movement is a grim and energetic scherzo based on sinuous chromatic motives and a lively figure in rising thirds, a colt from the same stable as the scherzo of the Fourth Symphony. The main theme of the slow movement (3/4 *Andante con moto*) is unusual in its 4 + 4 + 5 + 4 bar structure and in Ravelian ninth chords which continually defer the point of rest:

Ex.20

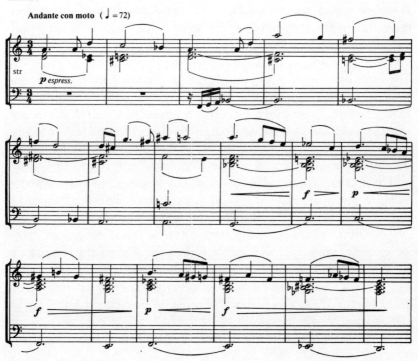

The last movement starts with a *sotto voce* march built on shifting
harmonic foundations:

Ex.21

A stormy central section is followed by a *meno mosso* recapitulation, a
running-out of confidence and energy rather than a triumphant
peroration.

The *Little Suite* No. 2 Op. 78 for orchestra, written for the Farnham
Festival of 1963, is carefully devised for amateur use. Strings are
rarely asked to venture out of first position, wind parts are
considerately laid out in middle registers (horns ascend to c' on only
two occasions, and then under cover of the full orchestra). No doubt
because the work is scored so that 'it can be effectively performed by
strings and any combination of wind and percussion available' there
is more doubling of strings and wind than is usual in Arnold's
orchestral scores; but the Arnold accent is unmistakable.

   The *Overture* (4/4 *Allegro moderato*) is a bold and bracing curtain-
raiser of the same type as the first movement of the *Little Suite* No. 1
for Brass Band soon to be discussed. In the central *Ballad*, two eight-
bar melodies repeat and alternate in varied instrumentations. The
final *Dance* (3/4 *Vivace*) is the most interesting of the three
movements: a country cousin of the jazzy finale of the Concerto for
Two Pianos (Three Hands) (see p. 145), similarly based on

major–minor alternations, the main theme supported by a rhythmic ostinato of timpani, bongos, and cymbal struck with side-drum stick.

In such works, written for young players for whom the whole world of music was still unexplored and full of promise, Arnold was able to retrace his steps and to recapture something of the uninhibited zest and high spirits of his own youth. There is no lack of exuberance either in the outer movements of the *Four Cornish Dances* Op. 91 of 1966; though these are rather more than the entertainment pieces we might expect from the title. There were no obvious models or precedents for the composer setting out to write Cornish music in the twentieth century – none, at least, for composers like Arnold who steer clear of folk-music precedents. Perhaps as a result, he was able to draw more freely on inner inspiration, to produce one of the most interesting of his dance-suite sets and the one that is furthest removed from dance roots.

Thus, it is perfectly possible, in the opening bars, to imagine fishermen, farm workers, and tin miners leaping vigorously to the bold and strongly rhythmic music of the first dance (3/4 *Vivace*). But they would certainly have been thrown into confusion by the overlap of the sixteenth bar of the dance theme with the first bar of its repeat. Country fiddlers would have been equally unprepared to cope with the downward modulation of a minor third at each successive entry of the main theme, so that at its fifth and last appearance the tune had moved from C major, through A, F sharp, E flat, back to the home key. The second movement (3/4 *Andantino*) starts as a hesitant dance, almost oriental in flavour, its descending phrases suspended against tenuous and transparent backgrounds, harp and tuned percussion being much in evidence. The dancer – always supposing there is a dancer – seems as diffident and forlorn as the Harlequin pictured in Debussy's late Cello Sonata.

The third movement abandons all connection with the dance; it is in fact a straightforward Cornish hymn, even down to the final *Amen*. It is marked by Arnold *Con moto e sempre senza parodia*; but there is surely a touch of affectionate parody in the excitable way in which the primitive tonic–dominant bass proudly calls attention to itself and in a final grand crescendo that measures the height of Methodist fervour.

The last movement offers a vigorous Holstian mixture of march and jig, then works up to a big and densely orchestrated climax based on an ominous side-drum rhythm in which we catch an echo of 'On Ilkley Moor'. The spirit of the dance has been transformed into something almost threatening; we have moved away from the village green and into Arnold's inner mind.

Music for Brass Band

In the *Little Suites* for Brass Band, both written for amateur youth bands, Arnold reverts to a direct and tuneful style and a harmonic idiom that rarely ventures beyond the occasional bracing and familiar diatonic discord. Thus, the *Prelude* of the *Little Suite* No. 1 for Brass Band Op. 80 of 1965 (4/4 *Allegro non troppo*) is concerned with bold affirmative gestures with brilliant fanfare figures for the upper groups of instruments, *fortissimo* descending scales for trombones and basses, telling contrasts between sharp *staccato* and smooth *cantabile*. The *Siciliano* (6/8 *Andantino*) is led by a solo cornet – with young players in mind, Arnold keeps the instrument throughout in the expressive lower-middle register. The final *Rondo* (3/4 *Allegro vivace*) deploys the full band in *fortissimo* unison for the first time in an immensely vigorous dance-like tune with occasional offbeat accents. There is a silk-smooth trio section for baritones and euphonium in unison, while the dance tune's last appearance culminates in a measured trill for all except trombones and basses. There is nothing in the least innovative about the *Suite*, which still contrives to be vigorous, direct and unselfconscious in ways that will appeal to any bandsman and to any audience casually assembled around the bandstand.

Little Suite No. 2 for Brass Band Op. 93, commissioned by the Cornwall Youth Band, was first performed in 1967. All three movements are in A–B–A form. The first movement (3/4 *Allegro molto e ritmico*) is an energetic four-part round, the first bold four-bar *staccato* phrase acquiring a second part in imitative counterpoint, a third in brilliant slurred semiquaver scales, fourth and last, an expressive *cantabile* counter-theme. The B section is based on an augmentation of the opening figure of the round, the bright sky clouding as trombones and basses give a new turn to the harmonies. The first A section of the second movement (3/4 *Andante con moto*), oddly titled *Cavatina*, consists of an 8 + 8 *legato* tune for tenor horn and baritones echoed by cornets, with a regularly syncopated *staccato* accompaniment. (The solo tenor horn takes the tune in the reprise.) The B section is led by the solo cornet, the tune punctuated by dark chords of piled-up thirds for tenor and bass instruments. The final *Galop* (2/4 *Presto*) with its flamboyant counter-theme and trio in broken rhythm is brass-band Offenbach, rejoicing in its energy and uninhibited high spirits.

The Padstow Lifeboat Op. 94 received its first Cornish performance at the inauguration of the new lifeboat station in 1968. A lively A flat quick march for brass band is regularly disrupted as it runs its cheerful course by the insistent D natural of the Trevose Head foghorn, irreverent younger brother of the ominous E flat foghorn in Britten's *Peter Grimes*. Time and time again the awkward note reappears, while the rest of the band plays on, ignoring the ill-mannered intruder; the effect is both comic and threatening. The joke is not kept up too long; well before the end of the march, the fog clears and the appoggiatura D vanishes, never having achieved upward resolution to E flat. Arnold was to invite this same augmented-fourth *diabolus* into his Eighth Symphony a few years later, the intrusive note persisting throughout the first movement.

11

INFLUENCES
AND ANTI-INFLUENCES

'. . . not only no Bach and no Beethoven, but also no Schoenberg and no Webern either. This is impressive, and no wonder the man on your left keeps saying "sehr interessant".'

STRAVINSKY ON CAGE

It is never too easy to place self-taught composers in relation to their contemporaries. Arnold, who learned more from scores and from the sounds of live music than from any teacher, escaped or rejected many of the most powerful influences of his day and absorbed ideas from unlikely sources. As an orchestral player, he moved freely between many worlds of music, becoming intimately acquainted with fifty-seven varieties of popular music of which most concert-goers and critics know little or nothing. As a result, he has never shared the intellectuals' almost superstitious dread of commercialism or hesitated to put to use his first-hand knowledge of jazz, West Indian music, brass-band music, and many species of pop music. In later life he has retained much of the orchestral player's suspicion of experimental music, while his allegiances (with a few exceptions) have continued to lie with performers rather than with fellow composers. He has shown not the smallest interest in the music of Boulez, Stockhausen, Penderecki, Messiaen, or other pioneers of the post-war years.

In youth too he was untouched by influences to which many of his contemporaries succumbed. No trace of Vaughan Williams in student works written at a time when VW was revered at the Royal College of

Music. The Two Bagatelles for Piano Op. 18 of 1954 – lean, purposeful, a little dry in manner – are the only works I can think of in which Arnold adopts another composer's idiom wholesale; we would be sure to attribute at least the first of the two to Hindemith if we weren't in the know. No trace of Britten (except in the Blake songs) and, more surprisingly, no trace of Waltonian influence. Walton was one of the composers with whom Arnold did keep up a close friendship, and whose music he has always greatly admired. Yet even when he deliberately set out (in the *Polka* written for the ballet *Solitaire)* to model his own dance on the *Polka* from *Façade*, it is only in the first bars that any connection suggests itself.

We can hear echoes of Berlioz in *Beckus* and other orchestral scherzos, of Sibelius in the First Symphony, of Bartók in the First Quartet, of Mahler in the Second Symphony, of Hindemith in many of the more argumentative contrapuntal chamber works and concertos of early years. But Arnold never followed in this or that master's footsteps for long, and was always more concerned with principles of construction than with surface mannerisms. The Sibelius-based development of *Beckus* has already been mentioned; there is also the case of the first movement of the Third Symphony, built on the plan of the first movement of Sibelius's Fifth, in which the opening 4/4 *Allegro* leads directly to a 6/8 *Vivace* which can be construed either as extended coda or as semi-detached scherzo. But who would have spotted either connection if Arnold himself hadn't mentioned it?

His use of serialism has also been special to himself, so much so that when he has introduced serial themes or processes listeners have rarely realized what he was about. In such cases, 'influence' is hardly the word to describe the connection. It is rather as though a door has been opened and Arnold had been given permission – or confidence – to go forward along a certain route.

On occasion Arnold will deliberately step inside a particular idiom – balletic, cinematic, or popular. In an age when creative individuality is highly rated, this is a risky course for a 'serious' composer to pursue. But Arnold, aware of the strength of his own musical personality, has never attempted to distance himself from his models by adopting parodistic attitudes. He writes from within the idiom, and *becomes* for the time being a composer of another species. Many

must know the theme song of the film *Whistle Down the Wind* which
went to the top of the pops in 1961 without having the least idea who
composed it.

Though he is at home in many worlds of music, there have been
certain tracks that he for long refused to explore. Like Constant
Lambert, he had no time at all for the folksong revival and deplored
its influence on English composers. 'I'm sure that the folksong
sounds, flattened leading notes and so on,' he remarked in interview
in 1959, 'are as artificial as a Tudor Tea Shoppe, and that the original
singers used *musica ficta.*' The folk tunes that Arnold himself invented
for his dance sets steer clear of flattened leading notes, the only
exception being the first of the *Scottish Dances* which is based on a
Robert Burns tune – and in any case, a Scottish flattened seventh is
not quite the same thing as the flattened seventh of English folkery.
Modal scales and harmonies are fairly common, but used in ways that
side-step the folk-music connection.

Arnold grew to musical maturity in an age when 'romanticism' was
a bad word, when Tchaikovsky and Elgar were dismissed by the
intellectuals as composers of little account, when Rachmaninov was
given a disparaging quarter-column in *Grove's Dictionary* (1954
edition), when the reputations of the diminished-seventh chord and
its relations were at the lowest ebb. In so far as he shared the common
mistrust of extravagant gesture, of attitudes of self-abandonment, of
romantic gush and more specifically of certain types of 'romantic'
melody and harmony, he was a child of his time.

The self-imposed ban did not apply to the film or ballet composer
who expressed at second hand emotions written into the script or
plot. But in his concert works, Arnold for long kept clear of romantic
gesture, harmony, instrumentation. Not only, I imagine, because the
idiom seemed to be discredited, but because in early years he either
did not experience, or else suppressed, any inner urge to lay bare his
soul or to write his autobiography, Mahler-wise, in music. Up to the
time of the Second Symphony he was a true classicist (though not
really a neo-classicist) cultivating attitudes of detachment. I have
already suggested that he hardly knew what to do with the ultra-
romantic main theme of the slow movement of the Fifth Symphony,
passed off in a semi-apologetic programme note as a cliché. Only in

the Seventh Symphony was the self-revelatory impulse at last allowed its head.

In interviews and programme notes, Arnold has sometimes protested against what he regards as the extravagances and self-indulgences of the avant-garde. Perhaps it is merely complicating the issue to speak of 'anti-influence' here, when he has simply ignored in his own work the innovations of the advanced composers (in playing techniques, in notational matters, in improvisatory or totally serialized music). Yet if the rift between Arnold and the 'advanced' composers had not been so wide, the rejection less positive and publicly expressed, he might have been tempted to experiment (as Bernstein has experimented) with additive rhythms, to challenge the many virtuoso performers for whom he wrote to move out on to new ground, to vary the constitution of the standard symphony orchestra, even to experiment further with the 'new resources' of the electronic studio. How far this would have been to his own musical advantage must be uncertain. Whether he is writing for the standard symphony orchestra, for the absurd instruments of the *Toy Symphony* or *A Grand, Grand Overture,* or for diffident amateurs, or working within the straitjacket of passacaglia or variation forms, Arnold has thrived on limitations. But to accept the arbitrary limitations of an invented system would never have been in character.

There were also more positive reasons why, at a time when intellectual, 'experimental' music was held in highest esteem in critical and academic circles, Arnold should have steered a lonely course, moving against the trend of the times. 'Music,' he has said, 'is a social act of communication, a gesture of friendship, the strongest there is.' Like Copland, he has deliberately tried to bridge the gap between the élite and the unlearned, and like Copland, has come under suspicion as a traitor to the cause of 'new music'. 'My view of music,' Arnold wrote in 1971, 'is that it should endeavour to express what it has to say in the simplest sounding way possible, so that what meaning it has is as clear as possible to the listener.'

Going yet further, he has expressed the unfashionable view that 'there's enough despair in people's lives and it's the job of the artist at the present time to give people the sense of dignity, heroism and happiness.' The desire to *use* music – for the lightening, even for the improvement, of the human lot, has always been present and has influenced the course of his development, setting him apart from those who regard it as their prime duty to keep faith with the *idea* and who see every move to win wider understanding as compromise or betrayal of faith.

Arnold's music has always been (by twentieth-century standards) direct, plain, riddle-free. As in Copland's case, no volte-face, in the manner of Henze, Alan Bush, or Cornelius Cardew, was needed to make it accessible to the masses. But the move towards simplification and the process of stripping down to bare essentials has continued steadily throughout the latter part of his career. The wish to communicate in terms every listener can comprehend has gone hand in hand with a growing interest in sounds for their own sake. Thus, in the long unaccompanied passage for viola in the slow movement of the Second Quartet, Arnold clears the ground, thematic action being reduced to an unspectacular minimum so that we can home in on the phenomenon of 'viola in action'. So too in the slow movement of the Trumpet Concerto, the orchestra is stilled; the short main theme, repeated without variation, seems to exist only so that we shall savour the sounds themselves.

Occasions and performers have inspired and shaped much of Arnold's music. Hence the appearance next to each other in the works list for 1970 of works as various as the Concerto for 28 Players, the *Fanfare for Louis*, the Fantasy for Audience and Orchestra, the Fantasy for Guitar, and the widely differing styles of the clarinet concertos written for Thurston and Goodman, or of the flute works written for Adeney and Galway. The bewildering variety of Arnold idioms and moods has led some to label him as an eclectic composer. I would say rather that he has moved through a bewildering variety of musical environments, adapting, like any eighteenth-century craftsman-composer, to the circumstances, needs and challenges of each occasion, while remaining always the same man.

12

THE LIGHT AND THE DARK

Sixth, Seventh and Eighth Symphonies

No one, I think, could miss the note of unease that runs through many of Arnold's later instrumental works. The musical weather has become unsettled, the once clear skies have clouded, the mood may be dark or ambiguous, harmonic and melodic idioms tend more to chromaticism.

It is tempting to reason that such developments indicate a 'deepening' of Arnold's own character, an abandonment of attitudes of classical detachment, an introspective awareness of darkening shadows in his own life or a growing desire to reflect the problems of the outer world in his music – all of which assumptions may be partly justified. At the same time, the context of composition should be taken into account and should make us wary of blanket generalizations. Celebratory overtures, suites written for brass bands and youth orchestras, will necessarily be *Good News* works. But it doesn't follow that abstract concert pieces with their dissonant and disruptive episodes must be *Bad News* works. Contests between positive and negative forces may be all part of the more sophisticated show staged for the knowledgeable, worldly-wise, hard-to-shock listeners who frequent new-music concerts.

Arnold's Symphony No. 6 Op. 95 was completed in July 1967 and first performed by the BBC Northern Symphony Orchestra in Sheffield in June 1968, the composer conducting. The first movement (like the last of the Five Violin Pieces) was inspired by the playing of

the saxophonist Charlie Parker. The Parker influence emerges in the
first bars, in scurrying third-based arpeggios that precede the setting
up of a persistent rhythmic ostinato which in turn provides a
stabilizing background for rapid and florid woodwind flurries, **Ex. 1a**,
and for sharp cross-beat figures, **Ex. 1b**, which give rise to snatches of
legato melody vacillating between major and minor tonalities, **Ex. 1c**:

Ex. 1a

Overlapping arpeggios based on the woodwind's opening flurries
form the background for a lyrical oboe theme, repeated by the violins,
which also makes play with major-minor alternations:

Ex. 2

These first two sections (126 bars in all) could well have formed the contrasting groups, one vigorous and active, one more songful, of a conventional exposition, and we could have expected a regular development to follow. But in fact we are already well over halfway through the movement, which is to follow no known formal precedents. In place of development, we now have a stretch of 72 bars, largely athematic and harmonically almost static, which can be divided into three sections. In the first, long crescendos by alternating groups of wind are superimposed on a background of *pianissimo* trills for upper strings over a bass ostinato. The third section consists of a single 28-bar crescendo over a persistent pedal E, two complex polytonal chords alternating throughout the crescendo. Sandwiched between, comes a literal repetition at original pitch of **Ex. 1b**, strings now reinforced by horns.

After the second crescendo, **Ex. 2** is recapitulated, again in its original tonality, on unison strings, the arpeggio figures now on woodwind and brass. The ostinato bass of **Ex. 1a** returns for eight bars as though waiting for some new soloist to leap into the breach; then the woodwind repeat their opening arpeggios *diminuendo*, and that's that.

The second movement (4/4 *Lento*) opens with a shrill B natural unison for upper woodwind which gives way after two bars to an ambiguous compound of harmonies, doubtfully based on B flat. A sombre theme follows, its despondent character enhanced by the generally downward direction of its two-bar phrases and by surrounding harmonies in which upper and lower instruments hold fast to conflicting tonalities:

Ex.3a

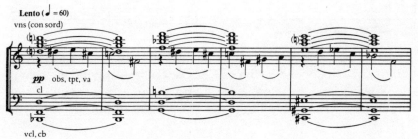

Ex.3b

The theme repeats in canon, **Ex. 3b**. Exploratory *legato* phrases, long-held notes for wind over a B flat tonic–dominant ostinato for timpani with side-drum and tenor drum suggest that the music is seeking a new direction. After **Ex. 3a** has returned on solo trumpet, this is discovered, unexpectedly, in a 9/8 *Allegretto*. Horns in four-part harmony repeat a quiet syncopated phrase over a percussion and *pizzicato* ostinato, with woodwind interjections.

Ex.4

The dynamic level rises rapidly with alternating scale passages from strings and woodwind, and a double crescendo involving the heavy brass leads back to the 4/4 *Lento* and the questing mood of the previous section; this time, the drummers' ominous ostinato continues almost to the end of the movement, providing a firm B flat foundation for the reprise of **Ex. 3**, again in canon and surrounded by conflicting harmonies. In the last four bars, woodwind, trumpets and strings in extreme upper registers reassert the shrill high B natural of the opening bars of the movement.

After this particularly sombre and closely scored movement, some sort of vigorous reaction seems to be called for, and Arnold duly gives us one of the most energetic and forceful finales he has ever composed. The often repeated main theme is given in full below. Its crude ebullience may well distress the sensitive, but its positive and arresting character is never in doubt. Note the extra injection of impetus from the accented tuba and bassoon note on the second quaver of second and fourth bar:

Ex.5

The aggressive character of this tune is explained when we discover that it forms the recurring A theme of a freely constructed rondo in the form of A_1–B–A_2–C–A_3–D–A_4, the three episodes all surprising enough to make the return to the terra firma of the rondo A theme both welcome and necessary. At the start of the movement, **Ex. 5** is twice repeated (horns and woodwind; trombones) before B, in which

athletic bitonal scale and arpeggio passages for upper strings, **Ex. 6a**,
alternate with mysterious *pianissimo* unisons in five-beat rhythms,
Ex. 6b. True to his usual custom, Arnold notates across the 3/4 bar
lines, avoiding a change of time signature:

Ex.6a

Ex.6b

Ex.6c

A bass figure, **Ex. 6c**, appears during B, which seems at the time to be
unconnected with all that has gone before. But when **Ex. 5** next
returns at A_2 (*forte* in lower registers) it brings with it a snappy
rhythmic figure for horn, echoed by trumpet, trombone, and unison
woodwind which provides a thematic link between **Exx. 12b** and **c**,
and **Ex. 1b** (in the first movement):

Ex.7

During C, quiet chords built up in thirds have been topped by shrill
repeated triplets on the piccolo's high C sharp, high spirits
dangerously verging on hysteria. A_3 is very brief, and is shared
between timpani and solo bassoon. D is serene: a thrice-repeated
eight-bar *legato* theme appears from its contours to be based in F and

inclining towards the Lydian mode; contradictory harmonies hardly disturb its air of ease. The rondo theme returns three times more at full strength (in A, D flat, and F) after which the harmony veers back to A major for a triumphant conclusion in which the tubular bells join joyfully.

The Symphony No. 7 Op. 113, commissioned by the New Philharmonia Orchestra, was completed in September 1973 and first performed at the Royal Festival Hall, London, in May 1974, the composer conducting. It is by a good deal the longest of his symphonies and sustains for most of its forty-five-minute length a note of high intensity. Arnold dwells on his themes with almost Brucknerian deliberation and does not shrink from exploring the emotional implications of his more expressive themes – in this, a very different man from the composer of the Fifth Symphony, who seemed to be almost embarrassed by the potential of its most eloquent theme.

The Symphony is not remarkable for structural ingenuities or formal complexities, its coherence springing from 'emotional logic' rather than from the interplay of themes. For which reason, it is surprising to learn that the letters of the names of his children, Katherine, Robert and Edward, are interwoven into the music of the three movements, and that each movement is in some sense a portrait of a child – the dances at the end of the last movement were introduced because Edward loved Irish dances. Whatever letter codes Arnold may have employed are deeply hidden in the music. and the element of child portraiture is similarly indecipherable by those outside the family.

Ex. 8a

Ex. 8b

The first movement (2/2 *Allegro energico*) opens with dialogue based on the brisk angularities of **Ex. 8a**, soon interrupted by **Ex. 8b**: a motive already foreshadowed in the first three accented notes of **Ex. 8a** (ringed in the example). First heard as a forceful unison, this motive recurs at several points later in the movement without ever taking on the character or function of a motto theme. A dissonant chord sequence for the harsher brass and timpani, **x** in **Ex. 9**, recurs several times and finally clears the way for the yearning main theme with its romantic secondary-seventh harmonization:

Ex. 9

This is repeated in varied instrumentation against the same syncopated background, after which first woodwind, then strings, fantasize on the falling seventh. From this spring further expressive *legato* motives:

Ex.10a

Ex.10b

Ex.10c

Angular and *legato* themes are redeployed and freely developed. In a short self-contained episode, **Ex. 10b** is projected against quiet chordal backgrounds. **Ex. 9** returns in jazzy dress played by trumpet with clarinet and trombone counterpoint (letter P) – a momentary relaxing of emotional tension, and the last in the movement. The jagged figures of **Ex. 8a** now reappear, backed by machine-gun fire bursts of *fortissimo* repeated semiquavers from all parts of the orchestra. A dramatic unison, heralded by a first ominous note on the tam-tam, suggests that a crisis is approaching. The machine-gun fire becomes continuous (eleven bars of repeated G flats, 176 semiquavers in all, shared out among the trombones) leading to a *fortissimo* syncopated episode led by trumpets, trombones, and timpani in which the whole orchestra becomes involved. Action is arrested by a threefold sequence of repeated chords given out at maximum strength by brass, separated by silences and heavy bass-drum thuds (a similarly striking effect in Copland's *El Salón México* comes to mind). Another massive unison leads to a resumption of the *legato* theme on full orchestra, and a free and violent recapitulation of jagged **Ex. 8a**, capped again by machine-gun fire which is itself cut off by three final, resounding, unison Fs.

The main elements of the second movement (4/4 *Andante con moto*) are an oddly spaced descending chord sequence, heard in the first bars on flutes and bassoons, and two grave *legato* themes which follow on its heels:

Ex.11a/b

(11b cont.)

Ex.11c

The movement opens with **Ex. 11a**, after which a quasi-recitative for trombone leads into **Ex. 11b** with the same chord sequence, **Ex. 11a** now in support, as shown in the example. **Ex. 11c** appears on unaccompanied violas, and is later taken over by a solo trombone which imbues this theme too with its own brand of *legato* melancholy and sets the emotional tone for the movement as a whole.

There are two non-melodic episodes. In the first, two strands of overlapping three-part chords provide the background for gentle tapping messages exchanged between bongos, tom tom and conga drum:

Ex. 12

The second consists of a *crescendo e accelerando* for full orchestra leading to a ferocious *Molto vivace* in which a complex and dissonant chord is reiterated many times against the same sort of semiquaver percussive barrage that we encountered in the first movement. The chords of **Ex. 11a** return, *lento e fortissimo* on full orchestra; **Ex. 11c** is heard as a subdued echo of its earlier self on bassoon and violas (tremolo, *sul ponticello*), the cellos and basses providing an equally ghostly counterpoint. Verbal description can give only a faint idea of the gravity and weight of this sombre movement, which goes about its business so deliberately and (incidentally) taxes the endurance powers of wind soloists to the furthest limits.

Arresting brass chords, **Ex. 13a**, and drumbeats introduce the vigorous main theme of the third movement, **Ex. 13b**: Schumannesque in the persistence with which it reiterates a single rhythmic figure, but saved from mechanical symmetry by the extension of the final leg of the tune to give a 4 + 4 + 4 + 6 bar structure:

Ex. 13a   Ex. 13b

The woodwind repeat **Ex. 13b** an augmented fourth higher; the strings add a new paragraph of 8 + 8 + 9 bars in the same style and then repeat **Ex. 13b** once more. As the music flows on in very much the same style and mood (again, very much in the manner of a Schumann finale) two more themes appear, the first involving rising octaves, the second, falling ninths:

Ex. 14a

Ex. 14b

As **Ex. 13a** is recapitulated, we begin to feel safely at home in a more comfortable and normal world than those of the first and second movements. But surprises are in store. The arresting chords and drumbeats of the first bars are heard *pianissimo*, as at a distance; after which a sextet of violas and double-basses sets up a strange rustling in the nether regions:

Ex. 15

For a time drumbeats, rustlings, long-held chords or single tones come and go, seemingly almost at random. Then abruptly, as though unseen powers had signed an armistice, the harp launches into a bland C major dance tune (6/8 *Allegretto*). This, it's true, is qualified by the alien harmonies first of muted brass, then of *ponticello* strings (**Ex. 16b** is superimposed on **Ex. 16a**), by a tubular-bell ostinato and an elaborate descant for piccolo; but the trite amiability of the dance tune is never under threat:

Ex. 16a   Ex. 16b

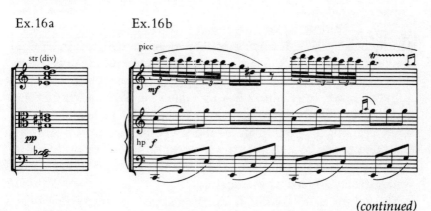

(continued)

The tempo quickens, and another innocent tune for flute and two solo violins sounds against the clarinets' drone fifth and tenor drum's ostinato, the piccolo continuing with its frantic ornamentations; **Ex. 16** returns for a few bars, to be banished almost instantly by the chords and drumbeats of **Ex. 13a**, and an exact recapitulation of the main theme begins. The end of the first paragraph has nearly been reached when violent dissonances blot out the musical landscape. Only variants of the rhythm ♩♫♩ ♩♩♩ beaten out by united drummers penetrates the din. The tumult subsides as quickly as it arose; two cowbells repeat the rhythm in their cracked voices. After a bar's silence, the Symphony ends with *fortissimo* F major chords and a final F unison reasserting the triple beat.

The Symphony No. 8 Op. 124, commissioned by the Rustam K. Ermani Foundation for the Albany Symphony Orchestra of New York, was completed in November 1978 and first performed in Albany in May 1979. It is the shortest and one of the most tuneful of Arnold's symphonies, the last two movements including only a few short episodes in which a song-like melodic line cannot be traced.

In one sense, the Eighth takes up where the Seventh left off. The main theme of its first movement is as 'innocent' as the folk-like dance tunes brought into the finale of the Seventh; and, once again, its treatment seems to illustrate the incorruptibility of innocence, the theme preserving its form and character under severe and systematically applied harmonic stress.

The nature of the conflict is clearly mapped out in the first bars. Attempts to establish D major as the home key are regularly foiled as G sharps refuse to give way to dominant or as the harmony slides away to the flat side of the key. Only the timpani stay true to D major. (Arnold, who stays true to the older non-chromatic timpani, here makes a virtue of their limitations rather as Brahms made a virtue of the limitations of the open horn.) Time after time, timpani enter loudly to declare: 'But this movement is *really* in D major.'

Eventually, and in spite of the timpani's protesting flourishes, strings, trombones and tuba all settle for A flat, and we seem to be poised on the threshold of D flat. But the piccolo, supported by woodwind and cellos (and, of course, timpani) enters in D major with a simple and symmetrical folk-like tune. Violins, violas and basses hold quietly to A flat:

Ex. 17

The sixteen-bar theme is at once repeated by the harp, the A flat still in the background. Next comes a tonally subversive theme in detached quavers for strings, **Ex. 18a**, which is soon ironed out into an expressive new modulating theme, shared between flute and oboe, **Ex. 18b**:

Ex. 18a

Ex.18b

The bassoons and lower strings take over **Ex. 18b**. First the harp then the timpani push for D major, but diminished-fifth fanfare figures on brass oppose the return (letter G in the score). In due course, **Ex. 17** does reappear (first on full orchestra, then on solo trumpet) in D major, against a more aggressive tolling background of seventh chords on a B flat–E flat bass (yet even now, because the tune provides its own inbuilt harmony, we tend to hear all else as off-key trimmings). The tonal conflict continues while all the main themes are restated, the timpani repeatedly returning to their obsessive D–A ostinato as if determined to bring the rest of the orchestra into line however long it may take. At last the timpanist gives up the struggle and we are back with the violins' and violas' *pianissimo* A flat. But the battle has been won. When the piccolo takes up the tune for the last time, the alien note evaporates, and the movement ends quietly in plain D major.

The second movement (3/4 *Andantino*) opens with a lullaby-like tune for strings, **Ex. 19a**, repeated at once by the oboe and followed by a chordal passage for trombones and tuba. At the eighth bar of this passage unison strings enter with a counter-theme, **Ex. 19b**, which is to play an important role in later developments:

Ex.19a

Ex.19b

After these themes have been exposed in various lights and various instrumentations the languorous mood is broken. Chromatic brass figures are projected against a glittering web of G major harmony spun by the harp, glockenspiel and vibraphone. The brass chords return with the string counter-theme transferred to tuned percussion, and the movement ends as quietly as it began.

The finale (3/4 *Vivace*) is a lively rondo of A–B–A–C–A–D–A form with three independent episodes. The main theme is not quite so simple as it first appears to be – note the way in which phrasing runs across the four-bar periods, and the dogged bass-line which makes its own sort of sense. At its second appearance a bar is unexpectedly cropped from the end, so that 8 + 8 becomes 8 + 7:

Ex.20

(continued)

The B section consists of four symmetrically structured chordal
sentences of eight bars each, the first two for woodwind, the last two
for strings, with a chromatic counter-theme added in second and
fourth sections. The C section is a free imitative dialogue of forty-four
bars for first and second violins alone:

Ex. 21

The D section (solo woodwind and brass only) opens canonically with
an eight-bar subject which is joined by two more or less regular
counter-themes. After the first three entries, voices fall away in turn so
that there are never more than three parts sounding simultaneously.

Meanwhile, **Ex. 20** has been heard in various instrumentations,
most of them lightly textured. The most unusual comes between C
and D, when the theme is given to the vibraphone supported by the
harp, glockenspiel and timpani. After the final double entry of **Ex. 20**
a few bars of vigorous D major bring the movement to an end.

The Eighth Symphony being a light-hearted work, it would be folly to
spend too long looking for the 'message behind the notes'. The
treatment of the principal theme of the first movement, however, does
deserve special attention, since the problem is a psychological as well

as a technical one. The movement marks a further stage in Arnold's continuing search for ways to incorporate naive material into the symphony. Perhaps the strangest thing of all is that at this stage of his career Arnold should have found himself facing very much the same sort of problem that Vaughan Williams and other pioneers of the folk-music revival faced when they sought to incorporate folk-music material into their concert works.

The innocent, 'High Germany' type folk tune is in fact Arnold's own, and first saw light in 1969 in the film *The Reckoning*. But it poses the same sort of problem as a genuine folk tune, which may be so complete in itself that it resists incorporation. Perhaps then the A flat or G sharp should be thought of as an antibody thrown up by the Symphony to combat that risk, and this anti-reaction itself provides the underlying theme of the movement. Schenker might have represented the whole movement as a chord of D major with a prolonged G sharp minor appoggiatura resolving only in the last bars, though in practice I doubt if many will hear it that way; we have become so used to multitonal harmonies, side-slip harmonies, appoggiaturas that resolve on to other appoggiaturas, that we accept them as part of the everyday fabric of music. My own impression is that, after preliminary disquiet, one quickly comes to discount the persistent A flat that accompanies the first few hearings of the folk-like theme – rather as one discounts the off-key hum of the air-conditioning plant in certain concert halls. In the end, the folk-like tune wins us over rather too easily, makes itself a little too much at home in the movement, and leaves us with a slight sense of frustration; as though we had met a charming person at a party who refused to be drawn, or to be anything but consistently charming.

13

ARNOLD AND THE ORCHESTRA

I find the height of my musical enjoyment comes in listening to a well-argued, thoughtful, lively and emotional piece of music played by a symphony orchestra.

MALCOLM ARNOLD

Some composers can be instantly identified from the sound of their orchestration. Beethoven and Berlioz, Stravinsky and Ravel, Chabrier and Roussel, Copland and Weill, all have their special sounds – though in Weill's case, the special sound was left behind in Europe when he sailed for New York in 1935.

Arnold's case in some ways resembles Weill's. When adopting a particular popular style or idiom (as in the Fourth and Fifth Symphonies, in the *Commonwealth Christmas Overture* or the brass-band works) Arnold will take over many of the instrumental conventions of the idiom. A rousing piece of film-title music, a ballet *divertissement,* a work considerably laid out for amateur orchestra or brass band, are orchestrated in very different ways, and I wouldn't guarantee that Arnold's hand is recognizable in every work. Yet many clues to his musical character can be traced in the sound of his instrumentation. His line of approach has changed little over the years, and he has remained consistently faithful to certain principles, which could be deduced from the study of a group of works selected from any period of his life.

'Clarity' is a key word. From the first, Arnold made use of clear, unmixed colours (doublings employed very sparingly except when increased volume is needed). Though he will sometimes make use of cluster harmonies or Bartók-like canons run at close intervals to create texture rather than audible counterpoint, his usual practice is to keep independent melodic voices well apart, while in polytonal passages conflicting harmonies will be segregated at different pitch levels or confined to groups of instruments of contrasting timbres.

The art of separation is as important in orchestration as the art of blending sounds, and is an art of which Arnold is a master. His fugal and polyphonic writing is always transparent; there are none of those busy but inaudible inner parts we find in the music of less skilled orchestrators. At the same time, his writing for full orchestra often has a chamber-music quality. In the opening paragraphs of the Second Symphony (see **Ex. 8**, p.46) every note tells; instruments or groups of instruments exchange roles freely according to the developing musical situation. Even the bass drum becomes, for three bars, part of the chamber ensemble.

Arnold, like many of the finest orchestrators, achieves his effects and his individual sound without resorting to extremes. His expertise is shown in the knowing use of instruments in every part of their range, in all permutations and combinations, at every dynamic, with every type of articulation, within the framework of twentieth-century normality. In technical matters, he remains a conservative. It is often surprising that so imaginative an orchestrator should also be so cautious. Double-basses are very rarely allowed out on their own, and are generally trusted with an important motive only in *pizzicato*. In his latest works, Arnold is still writing for hand-tuned timpani. No doubt remembering the uncertain horn playing of his younger days, he rarely exposes his horn players to the high-altitude risks that are common in Mahler and Strauss (the boisterous glissandos up to high notes are hardly more than sound effects; artistry or even precision count for little in this particular exercise).

Exposed solo passages for all instruments are commonly written in medium registers. The reasons I would guess to be both practical and aesthetic. In these regions players are likely to give of their expressive best, while the risk of mishap for the less reliable wind instruments is decreased. At the same time, Arnold seems to prefer the easy and 'natural' sounds and styles of conventionally played instruments to the strained and bizarre effects that can be produced in extreme registers. His avoidance of the lower register of the flute and the tenor register of the cello I imagine to be based on aesthetic rather than practical grounds – that he is (or in earlier years was) embarrassed by the inbuilt emotionalism of the sounds produced.

Arnold's note-sparing tendencies and his Copland-like preference for clean, wide-spaced textures are reflected in his avoidance of multiple string divisions and complex wallpaper-pattern decorative textures. There is also little shading by orchestration, as in the mosaic-like colouring of tunes by selective doublings we find in Ravel, Elgar or Walton, where (for instance) the cor anglais will join the violas for a note or two at the climax of a phrase, then drop out again, or a big brass climax will be built up by an ingenious dovetailing of horn, trumpet and trombone parts. Again practical and aesthetic interests coincide. A composer with as much work to get through as Handel, Rossini, or Arnold simply cannot afford to linger over every bar as Ravel and Walton must have done in devising the many-stranded instrumental traceries of their *tuttis*. At the same time, the passion for clarity and for clean, clear colours and bold effects also inclines him to adopt a lean, high-definition style.

In interview with Murray Schafer, Arnold remarked that the standard symphony orchestra was and would remain his first love, and also suggested certain desirable reforms. Upper and lower instruments could with advantage be reinforced, but the orchestra was already overcrowded in its middle registers. In particular, he found the cor anglais an unnecessary instrument. In fact, the cor anglais had already put in an appearance in the film score of *The Beautiful County of Ayr* and was later to play an important role in the Seventh Symphony; but Arnold's desire to clean out the middle registers of the orchestra was wholly in character.

His aversion to the cor anglais perhaps links with the tendency to avoid the 'expressive' lower registers of solo instruments that we have just noted, and which can also be observed in the Flute and Oboe Sonatas and Concertos, the Second Horn Concerto, the Second Clarinet Concerto, and in many of the orchestral works. Arnold similarly avoids emotion-laden *sul G* violin solos. He has remarked in interview that he finds the sound of the string quartet 'rather an awful noise, to be honest, with the cello wobbling away in the middle'. The viola is the only string instrument allowed to sing at length on its lower strings, Arnold having a special fondness for the instrument as a bearer of dark messages.

There is no explaining why one composer loves certain types of sound and abhors others, but maybe the fact that the viola had not been cast by earlier composers in the role of romantic singer increased its attraction for Arnold, just as the cor anglais's identification with ultra-romantic and often mournful moods (in *Tristan*, the César Franck Symphony, and the Overture to *Romeo and Juliet*) may have discouraged him from its use. It is equally possible that the low standards of cor anglais and bass clarinet playing in the forties and early fifties led him to steer clear of both instruments.

In earlier works, one can sometimes trace direct influences in Arnold's orchestration: of Berlioz, in the bold and buccaneering use of brass *en bloc* in *Beckus* and subsequent orchestral scherzos; of Sibelius, in the use of paired woodwind, often in thirds, and in the massive brass crescendos in the First Symphony; of Mahler, in the chamber-music scoring and more specifically in the treatment of the harp in the Second Symphony and in many subsequent works. There is something of Elgar in the Symphony for Strings and much of Bartók in the First Quartet; even a hint of Mozart in occasional uses of divided violas in accompaniment figures (see the example from the *Toy Symphony*, **Ex. 2**, p.126). In the later works, we are simply aware that instrumentation is at the service of the idea; or rather, that idea and instrumental realization are one. Not surprisingly, we also find that the more interesting the musical conception, the more interesting the instrumentation and that run-of-the-mill 'occasional' works are often orchestrated in run-of-the-mill fashion.

There have been some interesting developments in latter years. There was no precedent for the long and expressive trombone solo in the slow movement of the Seventh Symphony except perhaps for the brief but dramatic outburst in the Brass Quintet of 1961. The growing freedom with which Arnold writes for the piccolo as soloist may owe something to the example of Shostakovich; but it also reflects the appearance of a new generation of piccolo players who can be counted on to do justice to an 'expressive' solo.

As Arnold moved out into new emotional territory, and as his composing personality developed and matured, so the manner of instrumentation underwent certain transformations. He was readier in later works to mix the colours or depersonalize his tunes by sharing them between instruments (as in the Berliozian unison of flute and oboe at the outset of the Fourth Symphony, the unison of low flute and high bassoon in the slow movements of the Fourth and Fifth Symphonies). He made increasing use of tuned percussion and developed a particular liking for the misty, blurred sounds of woodwind shadowed by celesta or marimba (Fifth Symphony, slow movement, and many other later works).

While the use of much-divided strings in the Concerto for 28 Players can be explained by the nature of the commission – Arnold was writing for the English Chamber Orchestra, a band of soloists whose skills were to be fully exploited – the indeterminate sounds of basses and violas *divisi a 3* in lowest registers in the last movement of the Seventh Symphony are unlikely and surprising, and indicate that Arnold is by this time prepared to accept confusion and doubt as necessary elements in his work. Similarly, he uses percussion for the most part sparingly and discriminatingly. But he still allows brutality and violence their way in *Peterloo*, the Seventh Symphony, or the *Field Fantasy*, works in which the percussionists become agents of darkness, setting up impenetrable barrages of sound against which gentler elements battle in vain.

One further factor needs to be taken into consideration. 'When a composer writes a phrase for a performer,' Arnold has written, 'he should be acutely aware that the person he is asking to play his phrase is someone to whom the performing of music is just as important as the composing of music is to the composer. One must know the phrase is absolutely necessary to the whole work and that it gives the player the best possible chance to show himself at his best.' This sort of extreme solicitousness for the performer is rare among twentieth-century composers and does not necessarily operate to the good of the music; many of the greatest works have been brought to a difficult birth to the sound of the moans and groans of rebellious performers.

Yet the principle that every phrase must be necessary to the work is an admirable one. Arnold's respect for the performer, moreover, is practically reflected in many aspects of his scoring. In the Bartók-like precision of his notations – every necessary dot and accent meticulously and unambiguously indicated – and in music scored so that (as far as can be contrived) every part makes its own sort of independent sense.

Instruments are entrusted with complete themes, their characters rarely depersonalized by doubling or the fragmentation of melodies. The brass section, which in a good orchestra has the inbuilt sense of ensemble of a Welsh male-voice choir, will be used as a coherent and unified body so that its sense of identity is preserved. Arnold's determination to write the sort of music he would like to play and listen to himself, both sets the limits within which his music has developed and to a large extent accounts for its special character and for the character of the orchestration.

14

'ORIGINAL, SPARE, STRANGE'

Concert Works 1975–87

Gerald Manley Hopkins's words (from *Pied Beauty*) can without stretch of the imagination be applied to much of the later music. *Original*, in that whatever its function or idiom, its Arnoldian character is never in doubt. *Spare*, in that music is often reduced to its bare bones: in parts of the Second Quartet, of the Trumpet Concerto, and in the last of the *Irish Dances*, the slimming process could hardly be taken further. *Strange*, in that Arnold is increasingly prepared to explore the darker regions of the subconscious mind.

It is part of the natural growth process that a composer's scale of values should change over the years. In 1963 Arnold had spoken with pride of the First Quartet as his best work, which suggests that he felt a special affinity for the medium. Yet in 1975, shortly before the first performance of Second Quartet, he remarked that the reason why he had not written more for the quartet was that he didn't really like its sound.

The apparent contradiction seems to have arisen because the First Quartet was in many ways an 'exemplary' work; concentrated to the point of density, sticking close to its leading motives and working them over with much ingenuity. The characters of individual instruments were subordinated to the group character in the approved chamber-music manner. What was lacking was a sense of the composer 'in' the music, of characteristic Arnold themes and textures.

In the String Quartet No. 2 Op. 118, taking a leaf out of Shostakovich's book (Shostakovich himself having taken a leaf out of Beethoven's), Arnold treats the quartet as a group bound by no precedents, able to go anywhere, do anything. He finds room for cadenzas, for long solos, for cliché accompaniment figures, for 'empty' passages which have dramatic rather than strictly musical justification, for primitive simplicities as well as sophisticated and ingenious patternings of sounds.

In spite of the appearance of a rowdy Irish dance in the second movement, there is little humour in the Quartet and not one of the Haydnish jokes with which Arnold used to entertain his friends in the early chamber works. Textures are mostly open and clear, with little chromatic convolution or systematic working of short motives. There are long passages in two parts only, several unaccompanied solos; in the first and second movements there are only a few brief passages in four independent parts.

There are four main elements in the opening *Allegro*: hesitant scale figures (**Ex. 1a**); a fragment of melody which draws its expressive content, in a familiar Arnold manner, from alternations of major and minor thirds (**Ex. 1b**); a sombre and jarring figure for cello and viola (**Ex. 1c**); and the scales and gapped scales (not shown below) which form the basis for a vigorous and brilliant central episode:

Ex. 1a

Ex. 1b

Ex.1c

Just before the episode has run its course, the mood darkens as **Ex. 1c** makes an ominous return; the opening scale-based section is recapitulated, and the movement ends with **Ex. 1b**, expanded into a soulful eight-bar melody, *meno mosso*, in unequivocal D major, followed by a few bars' *lento* ruminating on its first phrase.

The second movement, the main part of which is in A–B–A form, opens with a cadenza for the first violin which seems to fluctuate between confidence and doubt as flamboyant flourishes give way to repeated slow glissandos with much harping on the interval of the augmented fourth. The violin finally comes to rest on a bare fifth (open D and A strings), then launches, still unaccompanied, into an energetic G major fiddle dance: a suitable offering for Hugh Maguire, then leader of the Allegri String Quartet and a fine player of Irish jigs.

The dance has run for twice eight bars of 4/4 before the lower instruments enter *fortissimo* with a fierce comment in C sharp minor:

Ex.2

With this clash of tonalities Arnold creates one of those 'sonorous images' which, as Copland once remarked, can pervade an entire piece to become an integral part of the expressive meaning of that piece. The conflict is fierce and unrelenting but also exhilarating, as the tune continues to affirm its spirit and identity in the face of odds. The B section is concerned mainly with static, rocking figures. When the first violin tries to lead his companions back into the dance, the lower strings will at first have none of it. Fourteen bars later, however, it is they who initiate its return with their C sharp minor ostinato figure, which dominates the rest of the movement. The first violin has the last word, with three solo chords, G major *pizzicato*.

The third movement is an *Andante* of unbroken *legato*. First the cello, then the viola, give out a long, ruminating melody, denied rest by opposing harmonies:

Ex.3a

A second, sequential theme springs from the first; once again, the harmonies dispute its message of apparent consolation:

Ex.3b

In due course a smoothly harmonized theme patterned symmetrically in eight two-bar phrases resolves the tension:

Ex.3c

After developments in which **x** (**Ex. 3a**) is treated in close canon, there is a free recapitulation working back through the serene sequential theme to an exact restatement of the cello's first theme and a quiet ending in C minor.

The last movement opens in Dorian D minor (no accidentals of any kind for the first thirty bars of 9/8 *Allegretto*) with an expansive theme for the first violin (the accompaniment figurations having been already anticipated in two passages in the slow movement):

Ex.4

Subsidiary themes appear; there is an intriguing passage of tangled counterpoints for the violins on their own. Then the violins and cello fall silent while the viola restates the opening theme, unadorned and at length. Arnold seems here to be inviting us to listen to the viola in its own right rather than as bearer of any important message: the skilled cook, weary of preparing elaborate dishes from exotic ingredients, asking us to savour the taste of a single fruit in a state of natural perfection.

This by normal standards uneventful episode prepares the way for a much more dramatic *Vivace* of sharp and broken rhythms, still centred around D minor but spiced with twisting chromaticisms. One outstandingly hectic passage involving harmonics suggests a Berliozian witches' sabbath:

Ex.5

Tension builds up through many pages of *fortissimo*; then, suddenly, the spectres vanish, and we are back in familiar country. The opening theme of the movement makes a final appearance in the major in grave 3/4 *Lento* and leads directly to a resonant D major close.

Like Busoni, of whom it has been said that few works of his really *end*, Arnold is often more concerned with processes than with neat solutions. In this final movement, not for the first time, he seems to be seeking a quick escape route from the imaginative world into which he has led us. We may feel a little let down by this ending, as when the last movement of Mozart's G minor Quintet leads us back into the common light of day after giving us a glimpse of the supernatural in the other-worldly *Adagio* introduction. But it would be a shame if we let our appetite for perfect solutions and nicely rounded-off forms stand in the way of our enjoyment of this lively and highly original work.

The Sonata for Flute and Piano Op. 121 was written for James Galway and first performed in March 1977 at the Cardiff Festival, Anthony Goldstone being the pianist. While the flute works written for Richard Adeney reflect a cool, classical view of flute character, the Sonata is closer in spirit to Weber's full-dress concertos and concertinos for wind instruments: in flamboyance, in wearing its heart on its sleeve, in its many florid decorative passages and regular formal structure. In writing this virtuoso piece, Arnold perhaps underestimated Galway's ability to do the simplest things beautifully.

The flute holds the centre of the stage throughout. The piano plays a subordinate role, though insistent off-key harmonies sometimes suggest that the conjuror's assistant has a mind of his own. In the first movement (4/4 *Allegro*) an introductory sixteen bars familiarizes us with one important chromatic motive, x, before the flute launches into the first of several ornate themes:

Ex. 6a

Ex.6b

The flute leads throughout the exposition and keeps the *espressivo* themes to itself, though the piano picks up a few of the flute's motives and works them into its discreet commentary. A development section largely concerned with x leads back in a dazzling flurry of scales to the shortened reprise.

The slow movement (3/4 *Andantino*) is by comparison simple and serene; the first languid flute theme is taken up by the piano, while the flute adds a melodious descant. The piano introduces a new rhythmic figure; the flute heaves four eloquent sighs before the first theme returns.

In the last movement (2/2 *Maestoso con molto ritmico*) the flute regains its high spirits in a lively, almost insolent, syncopated tune, which is anatomized to provide material for further discussion, the piano for the time being conversing with the flute on equal terms. The short recapitulation is interrupted by two dramatic hesitations before the movement rushes to its headlong conclusion.

But even the drama is playful – Arnold does not take the flute too seriously as a musical character, and keeps well clear of the darker more emotional lower registers in which flautists can reveal their Carmen-like capacity for passion.

The Fantasy for Harp Op. 117 was written for Osian Ellis, who first performed it in London in January 1976. Arnold had always written imaginatively for the orchestral harp, often in ways that recall Mahler's use of the instrument. Here, he draws eclectically on various styles and techniques, remembering the drawing-room musicians of late eighteenth and early nineteenth centuries and the French and Russian virtuosi of more recent times. But the opening *Lament* (3/4 *Maestoso*), which calls the audience to attention with big spread chords and imposing flourishes, undoubtedly refers to Osian Ellis's musical ancestors, the Welsh bards and harpists who were often also famous as sages and poets. A lively *March* introduces passages in *bisbigliando* (rapid repetitions of notes and chords shared between the two hands) and many passages in sixths – for some reason particularly pleasing on the harp. In a leisurely, Fieldian *Nocturne* a long *cantabile* theme unfolds over conventional triplet accompaniment. The 6/8 *Scherzo* goes in for cross-rhythms, and further varies the rhythmic patterning with occasional 9/8 and 5/8 bars. The lamenting is resumed in the *Finale*; after the final flourishes, E minor at last yields to E major.

The Fantasy for Descant Recorder Op. 127 was written for the young Danish virtuoso Michala Petri and first played by her at Wingfield College, Eye, in July 1987. Eleven minutes of nonstop descant recorder (longer than any of the Telemann fantasias) could well test listener as well as performer to the limit; but Arnold trusted in his soloist's powers to ravish audiences with the artistry and eloquence of her playing.

It is interesting to compare this work with the Sonatina for Recorder of 1957. While the latter tactfully observes the natural limitations of the instrument, the Fantasy glories in Michala Petri's ability to transcend them. Arnold stays within the recorder's 'normal' two-octave range, avoiding freak notes above c'''', always of doubtful musical validity. But the central *Presto* contains virtuoso passages of continuous semiquavers passing through remote keys at the rate of 864 notes to the minute, with occasional sextuplet passages to be played half as fast again. Arnold plays down the instrument's C major affinities and specifies dynamics from *pianissimo* to *fortissimo*, a range far beyond the achievement of most recorder players.

The Fantasy is in six linked sections; an arpeggio motive and a five-note chromatic figure provide much of the basic material. As in other Arnold Fantasies, the work ends with a full recapitulation of the opening section. But it is only in the brief coda that the recorder settles, for the first time, in the home key of C major.

The Fantasy for Cello Op. 130 was written for Julian Lloyd Webber, who recorded it shortly before the first concert performance at the Wigmore Hall, London, in December 1987. In earlier works, Arnold

had rarely cared to exploit the cello's potential as impassioned singer;
but here, though any suggestion of romantic gush is avoided, the
cello's emotional character is not denied. Arnold shows little interest
in technical wizardry or in the virtuoso's ability to amaze us by
playing almost as high, almost as fast, almost as well in tune, as a
violinist. Instead, he asks us to listen to the instrument in expressive
lower and middle registers. Like many of its predecessors, the
Fantasy is made up of several short sections, with many thematic
interconnections, and ending with a reprise of the opening section.

The Fantasy opens (3/4 *Andantino*) with a bold ascending arpeggio
figure which leads into a sighing, falling phrase, the pattern repeating
several times and echoed in the scherzo-like 6/8 *Vivace* which
follows. A similar contrast between upward-aspiring arpeggios and
an answering phrase which qualifies their confidence underlies the
action of fourth and fifth sections: 2/4 *Alla marcia*, punctuated by
percussive drum-rhythm octaves, and *pizzicato* serenade (3/8
Allegretto), both of which make use of transformations of the opening
figures. In third and sixth sections, both marked *Lento*, action is stilled
while the cello sings quietly to itself. The first *Lento* is sombre in tone,
the second, serene, almost hypnotic in effect. Its main theme, derived
from the second of the two opening motives, repeats twice without
variation, with one eight-bar linking passage after the first repeat. The
mood of calm resignation is unbroken by modulation or rhythmic
disturbance. The Fantasy ends with a reprise of the first *Andantino*.

Over and over again, one finds that in discussing particular Arnold
works one is drawn into discussing the players for whom they were
written. So it is with the Concerto No. 2 for Clarinet and Orchestra Op.
115, dedicated to Benny Goodman and first played by him at Denver,
Colorado, in August 1974. Arnold's own character and aims had of
course undergone change since he wrote the Concerto for Clarinet and
Strings in 1948. But the mood of each concerto, the style of clarinet
writing, the tessitura, the quantity of *legato* and *détaché*, all reflect the
styles and characters of performers for whom they were written. The
Second calls for a jazz-orientated player of sharp attack, piercing urgency
in upper registers, with a more neutral middle register. Arnold seems to
assume, as Copland did in the concerto he wrote for Goodman, that the

instrument's soul is centred in the octave between f' and f'', and does not
even bother, as Copland did, to ask for 'white' tone in simpler *legato*
solos, assuming that that is what Goodman will provide. The Concerto is
also devised, not for any jazz clarinettist, but for this particular sixty-
year-old virtuoso. Arnold is careful not to overtax his soloist with long-
sustained *sostenuto* passages, and extended orchestral *tuttis* provide
frequent intervals for recuperation.

The first movement (9/8 *Allegro vivace*) opens with arresting
unisons for the whole orchestra – strings, two each of woodwind and
horns, the timpanist doubling percussion – alternating with equally
arresting gestures from the soloist who shrilly establishes his right to
dominate the ensemble:

Ex. 7

After a series of piercing top notes, the soloist enters into subdued
conversation with an oboe. A boisterous *tutti* follows, then the pace
eases as the clarinet introduces a quiet *legato* theme, while restless
accompaniment figures suggest that the calm is not to last for long.
Soon, the clarinet is once more embellishing the melodic line with
octave leaps and trills. After a shortened recapitulation, the soloist
enters a cadenza via the triplet theme of **Ex. 7**, then improvises the
rest 'as jazzy and way-out as you please, based on the Concerto's
themes' (but Goodman, at the first British performance, went off on
his own without reference to Arnold's music).

A bar-for-bar recapitulation of twenty-eight bars of the clarinet's first
theme plus four cadential bars concludes the movement and leaves us
wishing for more. Arnold had hardly exhausted the potential of his

excellent themes, even if it was necessary to bring the movement rapidly to an end to ensure that Goodman survived in comfort.

The second movement (4/4, a briskish *Lento*) opens with a serenely simple tune for the soloist, repeated by oboe with melodic embellishments for clarinet, which then resumes the opening theme, but branches off in a new direction:

Ex.8

One of Arnold's familiar undulating motives provides material for a short *tutti*, after which the clarinet recapitulates the opening nine-bar tune. A *pianissimo* canonic episode for full orchestra follows in which closeness of texture and the very slow chromatic descent of the bass through an augmented fourth from E to B flat bass slows movement almost to stopping point. **Ex. 8** duly returns and the movement ends very quietly with a prolonged ritenuto built into the notations.

The last movement (2/2 *Allegro non troppo*) is in A–B–A form and is headed 'the pre-Goodman Rag'. It is based on short syncopated motives of manic energy and brilliance set against persistent crotchet bass and expectable tonic–dominant harmonies:

Ex.9

In the refrain sections, soloist and orchestra (including a percussionist fully equipped with trap drum kit, wood-block, cowbell, etc.) incite each other to behave outrageously. The clarinet plays, in jazz manner, entirely in upper registers; the horns chip in with extravagant offbeat glissandos (one of the few cases in Arnold's music where it matters little if the players arrive at the notated terminals). The B section consists of a twice-through statement of one of Arnold's most radiantly straightforward tunes which provides just what is needed in the way of contrast and relief from the hectic non-stop activity of the outer sections:

Ex.10

The Concerto for Trumpet and Orchestra Op. 125, completed in 1982, was commissioned by the Arts Council to celebrate the 100th anniversary of the Royal College of Music and was first performed by John Wallace at the Royal Albert Hall, London, at a gala concert given in aid of the RCM. It is perhaps not so strange that Arnold had never before written a concerto for his own instrument; the trumpet, like the organ, can dominate the orchestra so easily that the whole idea of concerto-as-contest has to be abandoned. In most 'successful' trumpet concertos (including the Haydn, the Hummel, and that dreadfully effective work by Arutyunyan) the orchestra does little more than hover about in the background and exclaim admiringly as the trumpet shows off its study-book tricks. Nor, until lately, have trumpets cultivated the chamber-music graces; the Fantasy Arnold dedicated to his teacher Ernest Hall was brilliant, noble, 'manly' in the traditional manner. The Concerto celebrates the smoother, flowing, *cantabile* style now cultivated by many leading players: brilliant but never endangering the listener's eardrums at high dynamic levels; sweetly expressive in *pianissimo* even in extreme upper registers. Even today any trumpet concerto is likely to impose severe strains on both soloist and audience, and Arnold wisely keeps his Concerto very short.

The first movement (4/4 *Allegro energico*) opens with a strong, striding theme that soon branches off into chromatics:

Ex.11

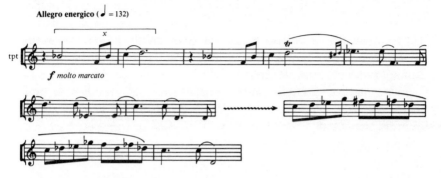

The orchestra takes up this theme with enthusiasm in a sonorous *tutti*, after which the soloist reproves its exuberance in a quiet *cantabile*, singing over the lightest accompaniment for violins and harp. When the orchestra takes over the *cantabile*, the trumpet in a spirit of contradiction reverts to its more familiar role with an outburst of brilliant fanfares. The short development is mainly concerned with the head motive x.

The trumpet is muted throughout the second movement (3/4 *Andante con moto*). The change of tone colour is welcome, and the *cantabile* theme (derived from the cornet solo in the Fantasy for Brass Band) displays the soloist in a new and almost diffident character; searching rather than asserting, with languidly drooping fifths suggesting that the high spirits and confidence of the first movement were no more than an illusion:

Ex.12

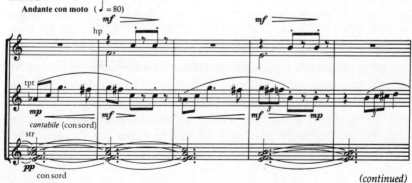

(continued)

The movement is scored with the utmost economy, the harp from time to time throwing in a hint of waltz rhythm, the violins and flute gently falling in with the trumpet's mood.

In the final 6/8 *Vivace* the trumpet throws off melancholy in a theme very characteristic of Arnold in optimistic and assertive state of mind, which also contains the very essence of trumpet character. The strings at first dispute the soloist's favourite B flat tonality:

Ex.13

An equally lighthearted theme in D major follows, taken up by the orchestra in another boisterous *tutti*. **Ex. 13** returns, this time leading to brilliant semiquaver scalework for the soloist, imitated by the flute and oboe. The orchestra breaks in, once more insisting on E major with all its force; the trumpet quietly declares for B flat, and after one more E major explosion the orchestra falls in behind the soloist, who tops the final B flat chord with a triumphal top D, backed up by the orchestral trumpets' B flat; a thrilling sound with which to bring this unpretentious and vivacious work to an end.

The *Fantasy on a Theme of John Field* is one of the few major Arnold works not to have been written to commission. It was none the less inspired by the playing of John Lill, who gave the first performance at the Royal Festival Hall in London in May 1977, more than two years after the work had been completed in Dublin. Arnold's interest in Field was sparked by the Irish connection. The two composers would appear to have little in common beyond fine craftsmanship and a gift for free-flowing lyrical melody. And, in fact, it is the distance between the two that provides the underlying theme of this strange work. As Paul Griffiths wrote in a *Musical Times* review of the first performance, 'The spectacle of Field (piano) crushed by ignorant might (orchestra) opened a sequence of images whose nightmarishness was in no way lessened by their grand romantic dress.'

Arnold summons up Field's music and confronts it with the (by comparison) grotesque and unbridled music of a later age. Extended extracts from Field's C major Nocturne alternate with episodes in which all thoughts of Field are banished. As Griffiths suggests, the Field episodes belong mainly to piano, the interludes to the orchestra. But the piano is also involved in a secondary role in the orchestral episodes, while the main theme of the Field shown in **Ex. 14** is lovingly taken up by the cellos quite early in the work, later by the whole orchestra.

Ex.14   Field: Nocturne in C

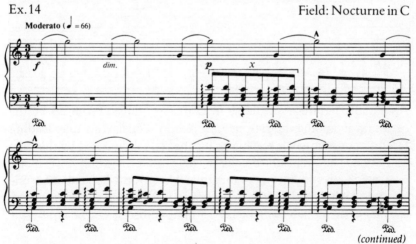

(continued)

The obsessive rising octave of the Nocturne also makes many appearances in the orchestral score, often serving to remind us that Field is still lurking in the wings even when the orchestra holds the stage.

A move-by-move account of the *Fantasy* would convey little sense of its emotional character or of the feelings of vertigo induced by violent stylistic transitions as we are whisked back and forth between the centuries. The *Fantasy* operates on several levels. First, there are the traditional contrasts between the one and the many: as when, after an extended and turbulent *tutti* the soloist enters with a calming theme of Fieldian origin. Next, there is the interfusion of musics from different worlds. A third contrast is between fast and slow music; the Field episodes all move more or less at the pace of the original Nocturne, while Arnold's two main themes (**Ex. 15a** and **b**) and their subsidiaries are quick-moving:

Ex. 15a

Ex. 15b

Arnold's own themes appear in many transformations as the work proceeds. Of the Fieldian material, **x** provides the starting point for a long piano solo in 9/8 which is almost an independent nocturne in its own right. At another point, the piano diverges from the Field theme into sixteen bars of an insouciant slow waltz. In the final stages of the *Fantasy*, there is a change of role. First, the piano takes up several of the orchestra's Arnold themes in a stormy free cadenza; then, in the final *tutti*, soloist and orchestra unite in a *Maestoso* statement of the Field theme.

Field, it seems, has won the day. But that is to oversimplify. We emerge culture-shocked, unable to escape the feeling that the Field theme will never be quite the same again after the adventures it has been through. The *Fantasy* remains one of the most disturbing of Arnold's works, all the more so because it offers the listener no clues as to the ways in which (rationally or emotionally) its message should be interpreted.

The *Variations for Orchestra on a Theme of Ruth Gipps* Op. 122 were written for the Chanticleer Orchestra, founded by Ruth Gipps and made up mainly of students and young professionals. The orchestra first performed the *Variations* at the Queen Elizabeth Hall in London in February 1978, Ruth Gipps conducting.

The introductory first chord, built up note by note, consists of all twelve tones of the scale, and is doubtless intended as a quiet joke at the conductor's expense. In 1975, Ruth Gipps had published in the magazine *Composer* a 'personal credo' which included the lines: 'For myself, I would rather die than . . . set down an example of "serial music". Am I right in thinking that every real composer feels the same? – and that those who do not are not composers?' The offensive chord is quickly cleared away, and the Gipps theme (taken from a Coronation March of 1953) is announced in straightforward manner, strings providing appropriate harmonies:

Ex. 16

In some cases, a composer may choose a particular theme to vary because it sets him thinking along unaccustomed lines. A late and brief modulation to an A minorish tonality would I think be hard to parallel in Arnold's own music, and may possibly provide the seed from which the third and fourth variations germinated. But it is the smooth contours of the opening phrases and the ascent to A flat that feature most recognizably in the *Variations*.

The first variation (6/8 *Vivace*) develops a new, modulating figure from the opening phrase, provides it with an angular and contradictory bass line and sends it journeying through varied orchestral landscapes. The second (4/4 *Alla marcia*) sets the scene with horn fanfares and syncopated accompaniment figures before the theme enters, in its original F minor but subverted by persistent pedal Es on bassoons, timpani, and basses. Arnold, it seems, is not out to give Ruth Gipps's tune too easy a passage; and soon it yields place to a bleak new tune, provocatively atonal (eleven tones sound without repetition in the first three bars).

This theme is carried over into the third variation (3/4 *Lento*), in which the original theme makes no appearance. The fourth variation (2/4 *Vivace*) is another march-like movement in which the second theme again plays an important role; but in due course Gipps arrives back, in retrograde form:

Ex.17

The fifth variation is a slow waltz in which the F minor theme again contends with contradictory E naturals. In the *Finale* (4/4 *Maestoso*) expansive unison string phrases based on x prepare the way for a shortened reprise of the main theme in the original instrumentation and an emphatic cadence in A flat major.

It cannot be said that, by rhythmic transformations in variation 1 or by running it backwards in variation 4, Arnold throws much new light on Ruth Gipps's theme, which functions, in a less disturbing way, rather as Field's nocturnal themes function in the *Fantasy*. Arnold establishes the mood of the original, indulges it, questions it, allows alien elements to disturb its pastoral calm and, in the end, allows it to win through; but the dramatic action has been too brief and inconclusive for us to feel that the victory has been a famous one.

The *Philharmonic Concerto* Op. 120 was commissioned by the Commercial Union Insurance Company for the London Philharmonic Orchestra's tour of the USA in 1976, and first performed by the LPO under Bernard Haitink at the Royal Festival Hall in London in October of that year. Arnold, with his great respect for the symphony orchestra as a fully formed musical organism with its own highly evolved patterns of behaviour, does not attempt any bizarre subdivisions and treats the four groups of woodwind, brass, percussion and strings in the traditional manner, as members of a close-knit community of semi-independent states, accustomed to co-operate on officially agreed terms, but also indulging in less formal liaisons. Thus, we find the expected contrasts in the *Intrada* (4/4 *Vivace*) between rushing woodwind scales, ringing brass fanfares, and sonorous unison tunes for strings, with a static episode in which interest is focused on the percussion; also less expectable passages such as the one shown below, in which the violins' *moto perpetuo* accompanies the horn solo over double-basses' seven-quaver ground (note that the violins have a diminished version of the main theme, and that the theme itself is palindromic, running back from the *fortissimo* B to its starting point):

Ex.18

This *legato* theme is the central and most memorable feature of the *Intrada*, recurring six times and in the process giving violins, concerted woodwind with glockenspiel, harp (supported by bongos and strings), cor anglais and horn the chance to display artistry in expressive *legato*. The theme appears in the first instance on violins against soft woodwind cluster chords, thereafter in various harmonic contexts.

The solo viola, in Arnold's often-favoured C and G string register, leads in the *Aria* (9/8 *Andantino*) with a sombre theme of doubtful tonality, doubts not resolved by the equally chromatic bass line. But later, the sun is to break through in a longer and more expansive lyrical theme for violins. During the movement, a trio of oboes and cor anglais transforms the viola's theme into a three-part canon; the solo trombone is given a chance to shine, the flute and harp effect a magical transformation of the lyrical theme. The more significant magic of the movement, though, lies not so much in themes or instrumentation as in the ways in which the narrative line is moulded so that the sound images of the instrumental sampler are woven into an indivisible whole.

The final *Chacony* (3/4 *Energico*) is based on a ten-bar theme first heard in forceful unison:

Ex. 19

The theme repeats, each time a tone or semitone higher, through an octave and a fifth to reach B flat in the fifteenth variation, with a final E flat entry to end the movement and the *Concerto*. The opening variations are loud and clamorous, reaching a climax of complexity and brilliance in the fourth. The next three form a little slow movement, chorale-like variations for wind and lower strings framing a sombre interlude for harp and flute.

Cellos and basses, combined brass ensemble, and solo trumpet lead the next three variations, after which the chaconne theme passes up into the heights on unison violins and woodwind. A prolonged unison B flat prepares the way for a final E flat statement of the chaconne theme. By now, Arnold has taken the whole orchestra through its paces; even the cor anglais has had its moment of glory.

The Symphony for Brass Instruments was written for the Philip Jones Brass Ensemble and was first performed by them at the Cheltenham Festival in July 1979. The ensemble, which had started life as a brass quintet, expanded on occasion to what was virtually a brass orchestra consisting of four trumpets (including piccolo B flat trumpet, giving an extra octave's upward range), four trombones, horn and tuba. Arnold, alive to the possibilities and also to the likely pitfalls in writing for this newly evolved ensemble, shaped his work to the occasion. Like other pieces of this period, the Symphony is a 'dark' work, but in this case the reason surely lies partly in the nature of the ensemble with its preponderance of middle- and lower-register instruments and its capacity for grave *sostenuto*. He also took advantage of the ability of every player in the ensemble to sustain long solos with conviction – the third and fourth trumpets are particularly well served; the tuba is given extended solos in every movement. The use of the piccolo trumpet as a solo instrument with a special character of its own is also worth noting.

What seems to intrigue Arnold most is the possibility for new *dispositions* of instruments; for Gabrieli-like variations of density and timbre, for the creation of smaller temporary ensembles within the whole, and also for the ways in which the *tutti* ensemble can be made to sound. As in other works of this period, tunes count for less than treatments, while Arnold, as though wanting to establish a new base of operations for this new sort of brass ensemble, steers clear of almost all the familiar clichés and turns of phrase in which brass instruments are apt to proclaim their ancestral characters. Particularly interesting is the free use of dissonances which the ear hardly registers as dissonances, because the timbres of the various families of instruments place them on separate planes of sound.

The Symphony plays for just over half an hour, longer than any of the orchestral works of later years except the Seventh Symphony. The first and third movements with their symmetrical and sequential repetitions are conceived on a spacious, almost Brucknerian, architectural scale, while the many long-sustained themes make it one of the most taxing works from the point of view of endurance in the brass repertory.

The first movement (4/4 *Allegro moderato*) opens, like the first movement of the Second Quartet, with scale figures set against slow-moving harmonies. The layout of the first bars shows the way in which the ten instruments are often divided: into balancing ensembles of trumpet and trombones, with horn and tuba in alliance taking an independent line:

Ex.20

A canonic motive follows, then a longer melody for solo trumpet, lack of tonal variety being mitigated by continual variations of instrumental patterning. A central 9/8 *Vivace* displays the tuba in florid passage-work; the movement returns to its starting point with a thirty-seven-bar recapitulation of the opening section.

The second movement (3/4 *Allegretto grazioso*) has something of the character and function of Brahms's gentler intermezzo movements. The full ensemble is never used, many passages are in two parts only. Once again, the tuba takes the lead in an extended B section.

The ground has now been well prepared for the most dramatic movement of the Symphony (4/4 *Andante con moto*). The piccolo trumpet sounds the key motive of the movement (**Ex. 21a**), which is followed by a forceful unison (**Ex. 21b**):

Ex.21a

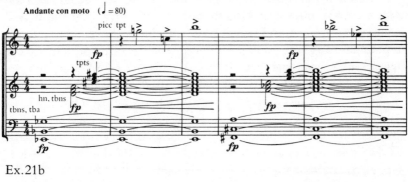

Ex.21b

In the latter part of the movement, the soloists declaim against
subdued harmonic backgrounds, the individual voice of the piccolo
trumpet often to the fore. Thematic connections with earlier
movements are present, but are not officiously stressed.

The finale opens as a 'double fugue', both subjects stated
simultaneously:

Ex.22

There is a double exposition, first for upper instruments, then for
lower, the number of contrapuntal voices actively engaged never
exceeding four. After a flash of fanfares, the horn initiates a lazy sort

of waltz. Fourth trumpet, first trombone, then horn again carry on with the waltz, after which the fugue resumes very quietly on muted trumpets, trombone, and finally tuba, carrying the theme down to the depths and leading to a brief reminiscence (still in 3/4) of the Symphony's first bars. The fugue returns, *forte* and unmuted, its principal theme finally given at full force and in unison by the whole ensemble before the emphatic close in the home key of B flat.

The Irish Dances, completed in 1986, stand further from traditional origins than any of the earlier dance sets: only the first, which is symmetrically structured in eight-bar sections, has the regularity of functional dance music. The dance theme, of the invigorating sort which makes listeners want to leap from their seats, is first stated on full orchestra; trumpets and horns lead the first repeat, piccolo (with harp in attendance) the second. The last two repeats are again for full orchestra.

The second dance is slow and serene, clear and 'open' in sound, one of those long paragraphs of sustained melody which it's given to few to conceive. Three-part string writing predominates: wind are heard in a single five-bar passage which recalls the opening phrase. Though there are thematic and rhythmic cross-connections, this is – unusually for Arnold – the only literal repetition in the piece. After the wind intervention, a *fortissimo* climax is followed by a protracted dying fall, with long drawn-out suspensions continuing till the movement's last bars.

The third dance is based on a wistful four-note motive, thrice repeated, followed by descending suspensions. This theme has close relatives in the Fantasy for Brass Band (cornet solo) and in the slow movement of the Trumpet Concerto (see **Ex. 12**, p. 207). The mood is that of a slow waltz; there is a tiny central interlude for three solo trumpets.

The final dance begins in the spirit of a jig with an energetic unison for upper instruments. Once again, the music refuses to fall into regular metrical patterns. The main motives are taken up, first by two flutes on their own, then by first and second violins, with full orchestra joining in only in the final bars. Textures are spare, the whole movement being in two-part counterpoint without harmonic filling.

15

TUNES AND TREATMENTS
Summary of Musical Characteristics

Tunes

Any attempt to define Arnold's musical character must surely begin with the tunes; the lyrical, easeful *cantabiles*, generally in major keys, of the earlier works, the vigorous and strongly rhythmic tunes of many finales and of the *English Dances*; the more convoluted themes of the middle-period symphonies . . . they come in all shapes and sizes, conforming to no fixed models. Many of the finest are also the simplest, created within the eight-bar framework, often of the 2 + 2 + 2 + 2 variety, often proceeding by regular sequential steps.

There are tunes that never stray from the home key. There are modulating themes that, in Hindemithian fashion, arrive at a new tonal centre punctually every bar line. There are tunes that start in harmonic ambiguity and arrive at a tonal terminus only in the eighth or the sixteenth bar. There are pliable themes, like the master theme of the Second Violin Sonata, which seem to have been born in order to be transformed. There are short and pregnant themes that are hardly more than motives, and *cantabiles* as long-breathed as the finest of Tchaikovsky's; one of Arnold's most remarkable gifts being his ability to create (in any genre) tunes that grow, like the *Pas de deux* theme from *Homage to the Queen* or the theme tune from *The Inn of the Sixth Happiness*, in a single indivisible sweep of melody.

In many cases, tunes seem to exist in their own right, and to possess identities of their own which Arnold will respect, repeating them literally, often in original instrumentation and with their own characteristic harmonies. Such tunes may behave like those characters who are said to force their way into novels, dictating the course of events to an unwilling author. The big tunes in the first movement of the Fourth Symphony and the slow movement of the Fifth resist transformation and become almost an embarrassment to the symphonist – unexploded kegs of gunpowder to which he dare not lay a fuse.

As Arnold grows older, the supply of radiant, lyrical tunes falls off, and we meet more of those apparently wayward themes which turn out, on analysis, to have been artfully constructed by the use of retrogrades, inversions, or other forms of note manipulation. Those who have typecast Arnold as a 'born melodist' and who listen to the music only for the tunes will be disappointed by such works as the Symphony for Brass Instruments, in which treatments, textures and timbres count for more than melodies. To get the most out of these later works we must approach them without preconceptions, with our minds un-made-up, ready to switch out on certain levels of attention, to tune in on others.

Treatments

Many movements are cast in the simplest A–B–A forms. Clearly structured rondos, passacaglias and variations are also very common. Some of the most satisfying of Arnold's first movements (in Sonatinas, Serenade, Second Symphony and other works of earlier years) are made up of paragraph after paragraph of melody, classically proportioned and balanced. Arnold makes little use of orthodox sonata form, but in almost all extended movements we find some sort of recapitulation, often drastically condensed, sometimes almost perfunctory, often consisting of literal repetitions of the movement's main theme or themes. Arnold, like any eighteenth-century composer, sometimes seems to feel that by the time the recapitulation has been reached the composer's real work is done, and the music can run under its own impetus. But the use of repetition in his music is of course far more than a labour-saving device. One of the ways in which Arnold declares his confidence in his themes is by repeatedly bringing them to our attention. It is also hardly an exaggeration to say that his forms are generally based in repetitive processes. The precisely calculated and almost classical balance of many of his earlier first movements is a balance of symmetry, in which repetition plays a vital part.

Arnold remains today what he has always been: a 'tonal' composer – though to say that is to say little about the variety and subtlety of harmonic processes met with in his music. His harmonic language is commonly third-based, seventh chords and (less often) ninth chords used freely in root position, rarely in inversion. Arnold rarely complicates his harmony with overlapping appoggiaturas in Ravelian manner, but often builds up complex multitonal chords by the superposition of triads or seventh chords. Polytonality and ambiguous modal harmonies may appear in works of any period. Arnold won't hesitate to fit out popular tunes with the harmonies to which they are accustomed if the context seems to demand it, but on occasion will qualify an aggressively diatonic tune by use of a semitonally displaced bass line or of contradictory harmonies in inner voices.

The balance of tonalities within movements, and between movements, is usually logical and clearly defined. Returns to the home key are often well prepared by pedal points, not always on the dominant – Arnold has a good line in elliptical modulations that bring one home by an unexpected route. It is not at all unusual for a movement to begin without any clear declaration of tonality, the tonal centre emerging only at a late point in the exposition. Sometimes it is only the final chord of a movement that tells us unambiguously what we are to accept as the 'official' tonality.

Arnold's feeling for key relationships is in some respects Handelian. Certain keys are associated with the expression of certain moods or emotions, certain types of popular tune will demand their own tonality, while in many cases the choice of an ensemble's or instrument's 'best key' will override other considerations. He is a master of short-term harmonic effect, engineering sudden plunges into alien keys as striking and dramatic as those of Berlioz. His favourite 'dramatic modulation' is to a tritone-related key. The sharpened fourth, both exhilarating and destabilizing, plays as important a role in his music as it does in the later works of Sibelius.

16

LOOKING BACK,
LOOKING FORWARD

Shall I tell you what I think are the two qualities of a work of art? It must be
indescribable and it must be inimitable. The work of art must seize you,
wrap you up in itself, and carry you away.

GEORGES BRAQUE

Forty years after the birth of *Beckus* it is perhaps not too soon to
attempt an interim assessment of Arnold's music and at least to
identify some of the questions to which we would like to have
answers. Briefly: how far have early expectations been fulfilled? How
far has Arnold achieved the tasks he set himself? How has his
musical character developed over the years? How does he stand with
fellow musicians and with the audiences of the day? How might he,
one day, stand with posterity?

Arnold appeared on the musical scene at a time when much
contemporary music was earnest, grey-toned, cluttered with busy
and diligently worked inner voices. He seemed to be the very man
whom concert promoters, publishers, and the general public had been
waiting for – a composer of music by turns tuneful, brilliant, and
tender; dance-like, martial, and lyrical; a composer who could give
'entertainment music' a good name, providing overtures and suites
suitable for Saturday nights at the Proms, symphonies and concertos
that wouldn't repel the common listener, but which would still
conform to concert-hall standards of proper musical behaviour.

This picture of Arnold as a latterday Edward German, Haydn
Wood, or Eric Coates, even as another Gordon Jacob, was a pretty

one, but left several factors out of account. The 'light classical' music of the past was essentially well-behaved; offended no one by experimental harmonies or by unconventional orchestration. It was 'happy ending' music: undisturbing, unexacting, often designed to be listened to with half an ear. Arnold has written works to which this description might apply and might, if he had cared, if his nature had been other than it was, if the good tunes had continued to bubble up in his mind, and if the times had been different, have made a notable career in this area alone.

But it is the prerogative of high talent to disconcert admirers and allies as well as adversaries. As those who knew him well could have foretold, Arnold wanted to choose his own line of advance rather than follow the line chosen for him by others. A composer with the ability and ambition to work on the broadest symphonic scale, who is impatient of the accepted conventions of 'good taste', whose turbulent emotions are increasingly demanding expression, is unlikely to accept the well-meant advice of those who urge him to stick to the job he knows and to continue turning out articles for which there is a known demand.

We were wrong, in early days, to pigeon-hole Arnold as a 'born entertainer' and as a child of instinct. I am embarrassed to remember that, in 1959, I myself referred to Arnold as a kind of musical Parsifal, able to cross all boundaries because he was unaware of the inhibitions and painful fears that afflict other composers. It is clear enough that Arnold had the confidence to follow where instinct led him, but it is also clear that he followed knowingly, aware of the resistance he was bound to meet, but driven by the urge to break out of the rigid framework of concert-hall conventions, to communicate with wider audiences and to achieve some kind of synthesis of the popular and the 'severe'.

In so far as he has worked to achieve this synthesis, Arnold must be rated an experimenter and reformer. Like most reformers, he made too little allowance for the inertia of the going system and the persistence of existing prejudices and *idées reçues*. Even friends and allies found it hard enough to *place* Arnold when he began to move off in a new direction. His publishers, advertising the Third Symphony in 1958, and possibly hoping for a four-movement *Tam O'Shanter*, came up with a little rhyme:

For Arnold's greatest work has burst
Upon us unsuspecting
With power and depth and magnitude,
And joyfulness infecting.

And everyone to Patersons
Is writing for a score
Of this his finest symphony
Bravo Arnold! – Encore!

Hans Keller greeted the same new symphony with an article in *Musical Events* (January 1958) in which he classed Arnold with Henze and Shostakovich as one of the '(at times) formless truthfinders' of music and pronounced that 'Arnold's profundity usually manifests itself in pseudo-shallowness, which is his historical inversion of pseudo-depth'. It is not by this sort of Kelleristic wordplay ('formless truthfinding'?) that we will come to terms with Arnold's work. But Keller, who rarely failed to score at least one bull's-eye as he spattered the target with bullets, wisely observed that Arnold accepted the most basic of a composer's responsibilities – that his music must make sense as sound.

The Fourth, Fifth and Sixth Symphonies with their more specific references to popular idioms were perhaps easier to come to terms with, to love or to hate. The sympathetic and anonymous *Times* criticism of the first performance of the Fourth Symphony in November 1960 is worth quoting at length. The work is 'addressed to the man in the street outside, bourgeois and sophisticated, musically Philistine perhaps, but a person of spirit, faced like any of us with the problem of living in a world over whose destinies he has no control . . . it is noisy, but behind the façade of rumbustuous extraversion the music is disturbed'. The scherzo 'floats insubstantially and horror-struck through a procession of nightmare'; the denouement is 'all brute force and optimism but achieves no real resolution. The aspiring pop-tune hero is swept away with the mob of band-besotted Gadarene swine and his high-pitched and passionate protest is drowned in the general hubbub.'

This does suggest that Arnold was getting through in some fashion to sophisticated as well as to simple listeners. But in the years that followed, the tone of criticism became increasingly antagonistic, often brutally dismissive. The big theme of the Fifth Symphony (again according to a *Times* reviewer) was reminiscent of Edward MacDowell, the whole work suggesting 'a creative personality in an advanced state of disintegration'. Jeremy Noble in the *Musical Times* dismissed it as a jolly neo-romantic confection about which 'the less said, the better'.

Every listener is entitled to his opinions as to the quality of invention and the validity of structural processes involved. I have already expressed my own reservations about certain aspects of the Fifth Symphony. But such total failure to get on to Arnold's wavelength suggests some kind of psychological block, which I would put down to three main causes. First, distress and outrage at the appearance of a composer who is willing to ask every sort of tune and idiom to his party. Next, the desire to slap down one who is thought to be getting too big for his boots – Arnold had already been typecast as hearty extravert and man of jollity. Third, the failure to realize that crude and obvious material may be subjected to quite sophisticated processes of manipulation, and that the presence of pop tunes or pop processes in a symphony doesn't necessarily mean that there is nothing else in the work deserving the attention of a sophisticated and sharp-eared listener.

Today, Arnold's 'experimental' symphonies of the middle period are more sympathetically received, or at any rate less fiercely attacked. But while the promoters of symphony concerts continue to serve up the same old mixture as before, it is unlikely that the new listeners described by the *Times* critic will get to hear either the symphonies or the more serious concert works very often. The ideal audiences for whom they were written, who can appreciate both pop tunes and symphonic developments, romantic harmonies and retrograde inversions, don't yet exist. Critics have no terms of reference by which to assess them, and even when sympathetic are apt to get the terms wrong. Thus, Hugh Ottaway, commenting favourably on the Concerto for Two Pianos (Three Hands), suggests that the 'oompah bass' in the last movement derives from Vaughan Williams's Fourth Symphony – the connections with the world of popular music which both Arnold and VW traded upon were simply not apparent to this excellent but blinkered critic.

The problem of 'placing' Arnold is one that many recent historians of twentieth-century music have bypassed by not mentioning him at all. Since history is largely concerned with the tracing of lines of evolution and with the work of pioneers, this is not so surprising. There is also the problem that Arnold – like Grainger, another composer of robust personality who 'composed with his ear' – bestrides the categories, and cannot be easily accommodated within the accepted historical or performing framework.

His music, none the less, carries within itself qualities that favour its survival. It tends to make its mark by means of strong and clear draughtsmanship rather than through the creation of 'atmosphere' which can so easily be dispelled or destroyed in unsympathetic performance. It avoids mystification and the sort of profundity which, in Valéry's words, is a hundred times easier to achieve than precision. It relies hardly at all on allusion to other music or musical idioms, on the knowing wink to the initiated. The more popular works are constructed, like Land Rovers, to traverse rough terrain – they *come off* in performance; they explain themselves to performer and listeners. If, after the holocaust, a group of self-taught musicians in Katmandu were to chance upon the parts of an Arnold work, of a Ligeti work, and of a Ferneyhough work, it is easy to guess which they would choose to put into rehearsal.

Yet though the music is generally so practically devised that it more or less plays itself, it doesn't always play itself very well. An Arnold overture or sinfonietta is not necessarily the easy, one-rehearsal option that some promoters deem it to be. The qualities of some of the later works have never yet been fully revealed. Nor will they be, until conductors appear who already carry the ideal performances in their heads before they mount the rostrum, and until players have become familiar enough with the music to be able to *interpret* the major works, rather than to give us plausible read-throughs.

A few enthusiasts have done great work for Arnold. Charles Groves championed the Second Symphony from the beginning. If the Seventh Symphony ever becomes a popular work, the main credit will go to Edward Downes and the BBC Philharmonic Orchestra for their magnificent and fully rehearsed performances in 1986. But those conductors who have made up their minds in advance that Arnold is a popular composer and no more can vulgarize the music as surely as they can vulgarize the music of Beethoven and Tchaikovsky.

In the case of the later symphonies and other major orchestral works, we are still stuck in the old *impasse*: until they are widely heard, there will be little demand for them; but they are unlikely to be heard at all unless loudly and generally demanded. There are, of course, recordings. Even though Arnold himself has remarked that records are as dead as Victorian stuffed birds, at least they have made many aware of the existence of music of which they previously knew little or nothing. But Arnold writes for live performers. Most of all in the case of the bigger orchestral works, we need the richness of live sound, and the stimulus of live performances.

In other areas, the situation is healthier. With an ever-increasing number of good chamber orchestras (amateur and professional) and with ever more adventurously minded performers seeking to expand their repertories, the smaller orchestral works and the concertos are not likely to be neglected. In the more informal context of music-society and amateur performances Arnold's music has flourished, and many have advanced with him into the no-man's-land between the areas of 'serious' and popular musics.

The number of cross-frontier works is by now considerable. Since the early breakthrough in the Flute Sonatina of 1952, with its innocent-popular last movement, there has been a series of lighter-weight but quite aristocratic concert works in which the learned and the 'galant' have been combined so naturally and easily that few have found the mixing of styles and idioms a bar to enjoyment. Arnold has often been described as a humorist and entertainer. But the value of the more popular works is greatly enhanced by their 'seriousness'. It is one of Arnold's main strengths that he is as whole-heartedly involved when writing a sonatina or brass-band suite as when composing a symphony, and that he does not reserve his deepest thoughts for important and supposedly serious occasions or equate *popular* with *shallow*. The *Song of Freedom* written for school choirs and brass band takes us far into Arnold's own psyche, while the blues movement of the Guitar Concerto is surely one of the most sustained and deeply expressive examples of the use of jazz in a concert work since Milhaud's *La Création du Monde*.

Conversely, the explicitly popular works often derive character and strength from expertise acquired in areas of 'serious' music. Structural processes, harmonic progressions and polytonal conflations can be identified in the brass-band suites, the *Song of Freedom*, the *Cornish Dances*, even in the *Padstow Lifeboat* March, which no composer would have hit upon who had not travelled far beyond the boundaries of popular music.

Throughout Arnold's career there have been no dramatic stylistic turnabouts. The harmonic vocabulary is used more subtly, but is fundamentally the same vocabulary in late as in early works. We hear the same voice in the Second Clarinet Concerto and Trumpet Concerto we heard in the Shanties and in *Beckus*. Resisting external influence, he has held firm in the face of widespread and radical change (often change-for-the-sake-of-change) in advanced music circles. But Arnold too, though less spectacularly, has changed ground. In recent works we can note a further slimming down of already spare textures, an enhanced appreciation of sounds-for-their-own-sakes, an almost Japanese economy of line in the musical draughtsmanship. Meanwhile, darker shadows continue to fall, with increasing frequency, across music landscapes once sunlit and serene.

The note of unease had been present from the first in Arnold's music; Beckus would be a much less interesting musical character if we weren't aware that he was a sprite with problems, perpetually at risk. Ever since the days of the First Violin and Viola Sonatas, angry episodes or blank patches of static, almost motionless music have from time to time qualified the easy lyricism of Arnold's music. But it is only since the late sixties that these dark and forbidding shadows have begun to spread, and that we have been forced to the view that this is more than a musical ploy, the artful use of *chiaroscuro* to enhance the contrasts in the picture.*

---

*Others have detected the note of anguish in earlier works; Margaret Archibald finds the interpolated *Alla marcia* in the finale of the First Symphony horrifying, and sees in it the reflection of Arnold's army experiences. I myself find the march grotesque, possibly macabre, but not in the least horrifying. The difference of opinion, however, is not over the existence of disruptive elements, only over the points at which they can be identified in the music.

The disturbing effect of these dark-hued passages is all the greater because Arnold's earlier music was, in the main, genial and optimistic. Sombre, static episodes now disrupt positive action; black holes are punched in the finely wrought fabric of the music; furious percussion breaks in and puts an end to all sound and sense. Sometimes Arnold seems to be scrawling moustaches on his own *Mona Lisas* in a spirit of derision, as though he had come to hate his own inventions.

When we consider how often he has declared that his great delight is to give pleasure with his music, that music without tunes is like religion without God, that the music of earlier Expressionists was the music of neurosis, it is hard to avoid the conclusion that in earlier times he may have deliberately censored some of the blacker, more negative elements out of his music, and that in such works as the Sixth and Seventh Symphonies and the *Field Variations*, they have forced their way in, refusing to be denied.

I recall Anthony Payne's comment on Schoenberg; that his music is so disturbing because 'few want to face what the conscious mind has been at pains to suppress'. These later works are often so discomforting that I can understand why those who have been enraptured by the carefree earlier works may prefer to pass them by. The Seventh Symphony seems to me to fulfil Sibelius's definition of symphony as 'an inner confession at a given stage of one's life'. But William Mann, writing in *The Times* after the first performance, wished that Arnold would stick to the task he was best fitted for: the composition of cheerful, entertaining music to make the world happier.

I note too that in the programme book for his sixty-fifth birthday concert in October 1986, almost all those who sent Arnold greetings harped on the bright and entertaining aspects of his work: 'Sense of joy in life and music' (Peter Maxwell Davies); 'Playable and enjoyable' (Yehudi Menuhin); *'Joie de vivre'* (Charles Groves and Peter Andry). Donald Mitchell, on the other hand, found him 'a composer whose unsettling disclosures of the human predicament . . . make him the altogether singular creator he is', and added, 'Malcolm's music often sets about qualifying its own happiness, and that is why I am fascinated by it'.

For myself, I would still be fascinated by Arnold even if I knew no more than *Beckus*, the sunlit Serenade, the Viola Sonata, and the Second Symphony – and I note that Donald Mitchell, writing in 1955, singled out as Arnold's salient quality his *unique recovery of innocent lyricism*. Could anyone at that time have guessed what lay behind? But the musical personality revealed by later works is more complex, more puzzling, all the richer for its ambiguities.

And the future? The general scene is a dismaying one. In the concert hall, the same old repertory works are repeated *ad nauseam* while the backlog of works that 'ought to be heard' grows ever larger as more and more fine contemporary pieces join those already gathering dust on the publishers' shelves. Yet in Arnold's case, there are outward circumstances which may encourage us to view the future with cautious optimism.

As we move slowly towards a freer, less exclusive and less rigidly compartmentalized musical society, works of mixed ancestry and genre stand a greater chance of acceptance by critics, musicologists, concert promoters, conductors, and others who wield influence in the world of twentieth-century music.

Perhaps more significantly, whatever the climate of critical opinion, and whatever the *zeitgeist* seems to dictate, Arnold's music continues to be played. Many good musicians, amateur and professional, know his work from the inside, often so intimately that it is built into their systems for life. Their influence may be limited; but at least a firm base has been established from which, one hopes, bold spirits will venture forth to explore the Arnold repertory further.

But the chief reasons for believing that Arnold's music has a future must be looked for in the music itself. Its particular strengths and qualities have been discussed in detail earlier in this book, and need not be catalogued again. It remains only to stress three salient points.

First, that Arnold (as Keller noted) composes with his ear. His music, however ingeniously organised, speaks to us first of all through its sounds.

Next, that Arnold is a positive composer. If some still find certain of his works objectionable, that is itself a mark of their power to affect and to disturb; like them or loathe them, you can't ignore them.

Among the scores of expert craftsmen of his generation whom we would unhesitatingly class as 'good composers' he is one of the few whose character is never in doubt. He puts on no acts, he throws up no stylistic smoke screens. He is what he is.

Lastly and most importantly: almost every work, serious or entertaining, carefully worked or dashed off at speed, tells us that Arnold is an original, without predecessors and without followers, virtually unclassifiable; offering us something that no other composer of his generation offers us. The best of Arnold's music is, in Braque's words, 'indescribable and inimitable'. Which is why (I like to believe) it will for long be played, and listened to, with wonder and delight.

WORKS INDEX

Guitar, op.67 83-5, 135, 227	P
Harmonica, op.46 80-81, 83	P
Horn, no.1, op.11 31-32, 82	L
no.2, op.58 82-83, 190	P
Oboe, op.39 34-5	P
Organ, op.47 81-2	P
Piano: Duet, op.32 33-34	L
2 Pianos (three hands), op.104 6, 144-7, 160, 225	F
Fantasy on a Theme of John Field, op.116 7,192,209-211,212, 229	F
Recorder, op.133 7	F
Trumpet, op.125 7, 131,168,194, 206-9, 218, 228	F
Viola, op.108 6, 149-154	F
2 Violins, op.77 141-3	F

Brass Band

Fantasy, op.114 131, 207, 218	H
Little Suite no.1, op.80 160, 162	P
Little Suite no.2, op.93 162-3	H
The Padstow Lifeboat, op.94 6, 133, 163, 228	H

Other Ensemble Music

Divertimento for fl,cl,bn, op.37 20, 30-31	P
Duo for flute and viola, op.10 20, 22-23	F
Duo for two cellos, op.85 132	N
Fanfare for Louis 132, 168	Studio Music
Oboe Quartet, op.61 77-78	F
Piano Trio, op.54 76-77	P
Quintet (fl,vn,va,hn,bn), op.7 20-21	P
Quintet for Brass, op.73 78-9, 87,191	P
Quintet for Wind, op.2 (lost) 10	
String Quartets: Phantasy, op.8 10	
no.1, op.23 19, 26-8, 165, 191,194	L
no.2, op.118 7, 168, 194-200,216	F
Symphony for Brass, op.123 7, 132 215-218, 220,	F
Three Shanties for wind quintet, op.4 5, 14-16, 29, 31, 228	P (and Fischer)
Trevelyan Suite, op.96 135-6	F (and Emerson)

Duos with Piano

Five Pieces for Violin and Piano, op.84 69, 133-5, 169	F
Sonatina for Clarinet and Piano, op.29 29-30	L
Sonata for Flute and Piano (1942) 12	
Sonata for Flute and Piano, op.121 200-201	F
Sonatina for Flute and Piano, op.19 29-30, 79,227	L
Sonatina for Oboe and Piano, op.28 29-30	L
Sonatina for Recorder and Piano, op.41 29, 74-5	P
Sonata for Viola and Piano, op.17 19, 23, 25-6, 228,230	L
Sonata no.1 for Violin and Piano, op.15 19, 23-5, 75, 228	L
Sonata no.2 for Violin and Piano, op.43 75-7, 219	P

Solo Instrument

Eight Children's Pieces for Piano, op.36 131-2	L
Fantasy for Bassoon, op.86 129-130	F
Fantasy for Cello, op.130 202-203	F
Fantasy for Clarinet, op.87 129-130	F
Fantasy for Flute, op.89 129-130	F
Fantasy for Guitar, op.107 135,168	F
Fantasy for Harp, op.117 201-202	F
Fantasy for Horn, op.88 129-130	F
Fantasy for Oboe, op.61 129-130	F
Fantasy for Descant Recorder, op.127 7, 202	F
Fantasy for Trombone, op.101 131	F
Fantasy for Trumpet, op.100 130	F
Fantasy for Tuba, op.102 131	F
Piano Sonata (1942) 10-12, 14	Roberton
Two Bagatelles for Piano, op.18 165	

Ballet

Electra, op.79 71-72	
Homage to the Queen, op.42 4, 66-8, 83, 219	

Publishers: F, Faber; P, Paterson; L, Lengnick; H, Henrees; B & C, British & Continental;
OUP, Oxford.

GENERAL INDEX